The Trade and Tariff Act of 1984

Trade Policy in the Reagan Administration

Stephen L. Lande
Manchester Associates, Ltd.

Craig VanGrasstek
VanGrasstek Communications

Lexington Books
D.C. Heath and Company/Lexington, Massachusetts/Toronto

Library of Congress Cataloging-in-Publication Data

Lande, Stephen L.
    The Trade and Tariff Act of 1984.

    Includes index.
    1. Foreign trade regulation—United States.   2. Tariff—Law and legislation—United States.
    I. VanGrasstek, Craig.   II. Title.
KF1976.L27 1986   343.74'087   85-45571
ISBN 0-669-12007-3 (alk. paper)   347.30387

Published simultaneously in Canada
Printed in the United States of America
Casebound International Standard Book Number: 0-669-12007-3
Library of Congress Catalog Card Number: 85-45571

The paper used in this publication meets the minimum requirements of American National Standard for Information Sciences—Permanence of Paper for Printed Library Materials, ANSI Z39.48-1984.
∞ ™

The last numbers on the right below indicate the number and date of printing.

10 9 8 7 6 5 4 3 2

95 94 93 92 91 90 89 88 87

Contents

Tables and Figures   vii

Acknowledgments   ix

1. The Significance of the Trade and Tariff Act of 1984   1

    The Historical Development of U.S. Trade Policy   3
    U.S. Trade Policy within the GATT System   8
    Overview of the TTA   12

Part I   Negotiating Objectives and Authority   25

2. U.S. Negotiating Objectives: Reciprocity and Retaliation   27

    The New Issues   27
    Reciprocity and Retaliation   35
    Section 301   41
    Section 301 and the New Issues   47
    Other Provisions of the Act   50
    Impact of the TTA's Provisions   54

3. Bilateral Negotiating Authority   57

    Genesis of the U.S.–Israeli FTA   57
    How the FTA Mechanism Works   59
    Provisions of the U.S.–Israeli FTA   60
    Significance of the FTA Authority   64

4. Renewal of the Generalized System of Preferences: Neoreciprocity and the Newly Industrialized Countries   69

    The GSP before 1984   69
    The GSP Renewal Fight   76
    The New Negotiability of the GSP   78
    Changes in Country and Product Eligibility   83
    Administrative Changes in the Program   87
    Agricultural Exports   88

Part II   Trade-Remedy Laws   93

5.   The Escape Clause   95

The Escape Clause and the GATT   95
Section 201   96
The Standards for Providing Relief   99
Available Remedies   101
Past Experience in Escape-Clause Cases   102
How the TTA Changes the Escape Clause   103

6.   Countervailing and Antidumping Duties   107

U.S. Trade-Remedy Laws and the GATT   108
Flow of Trade-Remedy Proceedings   111
Initiation of Cases   116
Injury Investigations of the USITC   120
Investigations by the ITA   123
Additional Rules, Procedures, and Definitions   128
Suspension and Termination   130
Assessment and Payment of Duties   133
Judicial Review   134
Administrative Review and Revocation   135

Part III   Other Provisions of the TTA   141

7.   Steel Import Relief and Other Specific Product Measures 143

The Steel Import Stabilization Act of 1984   143
Other Specific Product Measures   150
Customs Measures   151

8.   Conclusions and Developments since 1984   153

Trade Policy at a Crossroads?   153
The Repoliticization of Trade Policy   154
Trade Policy Initiatives in the 99th Congress   157
Conclusion   162

Index   164

About the Authors   168

Tables and Figures

Tables

1-1. U.S. Tariff Rates, 1789–1984   4

1-2. Principal U.S. Trade-Remedy Laws   17

2-1. U.S. Trade Balances in Goods and Services   28

3-1. Staged Duty Reductions in the U.S.–Israeli Free Trade Area   61

4-1. U.S. Imports for Consumption from GSP Beneficiary Countries, by Country Group, 1984   73

4-2. Results of the Annual GSP Reviews of U.S. Imports, 1981–1984   74

4-3. CNL Exclusions In Force, by Country, Following the 1984 GSP Review   82

6-1. Summary of Antidumping and Countervailing Duty Cases in 1984   116

6-2. Countervailing Duty and Antidumping Orders In Effect as of December 31, 1984   117

7-1. Share of Apparent U.S. Consumption of Carbon Steel Imports, 1984, and Voluntary Restraint Agreement Limits   148

Figures

6-1. Statutory Timetable for Antidumping Investigations   113

6-2. Statutory Timetable for Countervailing Duty Investigations 114

Acknowledgments

T he publication of this book would not have been possible without the encouragement and constructive criticism we have received from our colleagues in the Washington trade policy community. Past and present officials in the Office of the U.S. Trade Representative providing us with the benefit of their observations include Jeanne Archibald, Judy Bello, Charley Blum, Doral Cooper, Tom St.Maxens, and Dave Shark. Our layman's understanding of the intricacies of U.S. trade law was assisted by the counsel of trade lawyers Charlene Barshefsky, Shirley Coffield, Dennis James, Gary Horlick, Dave Serko, Laurence Schneider, and Sheri Singer. Susan Haggerty of the U.S. Department of Commerce, and Jeri Jensen of the U.S. International Trade Commission (USITC) shared their insights on U.S. trade-remedy laws and processes with us. We also owe a debt of gratitude to Ted Moran of the Landegger Program in International Business Diplomacy of Georgetown University, Linda Marshall of Manchester Associates, and Hal Sundstrom of the USITC for their invaluable assistance in making this book possible.

Most of all, we would like to dedicate this book to our families, who have endured our irregular schedules, cancelled appointments, and chronic absenteeism.

While we acknowledge the assistance we have received, any errors that remain in the book are entirely our own.

1
The Significance of the Trade and Tariff Act of 1984

The Trade and Tariff Act of 1984 (TTA) is the newest addition to the corpus of U.S. trade legislation, and will help set the tone for the next decade of U.S. trade policy.[1] As we explain in the chapters that follow, the TTA addresses many (though certainly not all) of the most pressing trade issues in the United States.

This book describes the origins, provisions, and significance of the TTA. The first chapter provides an introduction to the historical evolution of the U.S. trade policy environment, centering on the development of a liberal system based on a global view of American interests, the political dominance of the executive branch, low tariff protection, and a quasi-juridical system of trade-remedy laws. The TTA does not represent a dramatic departure from this system. Because the majority of its key provisions are amendments to earlier trade laws, most of the changes that it makes are incremental rather than radical.

These changes are described under three general headings, which together form the body of this book. The first of these is the negotiating objectives and authority that the TTA provides for the executive branch. The legislation endorses the Reagan administration's objectives in certain so-called new issues that have not previously been addressed comprehensively, but does not provide sweeping negotiating authority that the executive branch can use to achieve these goals. In lieu of explicit congressional approval to enter into a new round of multilateral trade negotiations, the TTA strengthens the retaliatory powers of the executive branch, provides for bilateral negotiations, and allows the Generalized System of Preferences to be used in order to extract concessions from its beneficiary developing countries.

The second broad area covered by the act is the trade-remedy statutes, which provide domestic industries with a quasi-juridical means of restricting foreign competition that is deemed to be unfair and/or injurious. The TTA slightly amends the criteria for finding serious injury in escape-clause cases, and clarifies the congressional override of presidential decisions, but these changes are not expected to alter the law significantly. The act extensively amends the U.S. antisubsidy and antidumping statutes. Most of the amendments are intended to clarify and streamline the operation of the laws, which had been made increasingly difficult to administer by the proliferation of petitions and ever more complex procedures. Some will have the effect of favoring domestic petitioners over foreign respondents.

The third category in the TTA consists of measures aimed at specific products or sectors, as well as miscellaneous provisions relating to the powers and duties of the U.S. Customs Service. The most important section within this third category is the Steel Import Stabilization Act of 1984, which establishes authority for a five-year import restriction program for the steel industry.

The concluding chapter of the book discusses the overall significance of the TTA, and the prospects for U.S. trade policy in the near term. It emphasizes that the TTA is neither the first nor the last word on U.S. trade laws, policies, or practices, and that trade is one of the more politically volatile issues of the second Reagan term. Depending on the political wisdom within the White House, the Congress, and the leading members of the global trading community, the next several years could mark a period of reinvigoration or regression for the GATT system of multilateral and liberal trade relations.

It is important to note what this book does *not* attempt to do. We have chosen to focus our inquiry on those topics that are dealt with in the TTA. This encompasses most of the central issues involved in trade negotiations and import restrictions, but leaves out most of the export side of the trade policy equation. Beyond the value of the dollar, the central export issues of the 1980s are the restrictions imposed by foreign governments on U.S. products, U.S. restrictions on textile imports, the financial and promotional efforts undertaken by the United States, the use of embargoes as a tool of foreign policy, and controls on the exportation of advanced technologies to the Soviet bloc or other potential adversaries. Only the first of these issues is addressed by the TTA, as discussed in chapter 2 of this book. The other topics are the subject of such varied legislation as the authorizations and appropriations for the Export–Import Bank and the Commodities Credit Corporation, the PL-480 (Food for Peace) program and other foreign assistance projects, the Trading with the Enemy Act of 1917 (as amended), and the Export Administration Amendments Act of 1985.

The book does not comprehensively discuss certain aspects of U.S. import policies that are not affected by the TTA. One of these is the special regime for textile and apparel imports, most of which are governed by the Multi Fiber Arrangement and the several bilateral restraint agreements that have been negotiated under its auspices. The special international arrangements for trade in coffee, sugar, cocoa, and petroleum are also outside the scope of our inquiry. U.S. trade policy is further punctuated by several formal and informal arrangements that are intended to restrict trade, such as the voluntary export restraints on Japanese automobiles. Neither the TTA nor the book deal with these issues. Although some provisions of the TTA address the micromanagement of imports, as exercised by the U.S. Customs Service, we have chosen to discuss only those issues that have a significant impact on trade policy.

Finally, macroeconomic issues are outside the scope of this volume. Business cycles, capital transfers, and the value of the dollar are ultimately of greater influence on trade than the legal and political underpinnings of the system, but they are not subject to the direct control of statesmen, legislators, or trade consultants—despite any claims to the contrary. We have restricted our discussion to those issues that can realistically be addressed by the legislative process.

The Historical Development of U.S. Trade Policy

In order to understand the true significance of the TTA, it is necessary to define its place in the history of U.S. trade policy. At the risk of generalization, the development of policy can be reduced to three broad trends: the gradual internationalization of American interests, the transfer of political ascendancy from the legislative to the executive branch, and the shift from high tariff protection to a liberal trading order based on the rule of domestic and international law. We will now briefly discuss these trends.

Although modern trade relations are in the province of foreign policy, trade was almost exclusively considered a domestic issue during the nineteenth century. In an era of political and economic isolationism, trade policy involved little more than adjusting the tariff to suit the needs of protected industries and government finances.

The evolving history of U.S. tariff rates can be seen in table 1-1. Import duties were the principal source of revenue for the federal government in the early years of the republic. Protective tariffs played an important role in the development strategies of Alexander Hamilton and Henry Clay, who extolled the virtues of protecting infant American industries from European competition. The War of 1812 further encouraged the escalation of tariffs, first in order to finance the war effort, and later to continue the protection that U.S. textile mills had enjoyed while trade with Britain was suspended. Following the war, the tariff became nearly as contentious an issue as slavery between the protectionist North and the South, which sought free trade. The Civil War resolved this issue decisively. For the rest of the nineteenth century, the "war tariff" established in the 1860s remained at confiscatory levels for many products.

As a revenue instrument, the tariff was the exclusive domain of the Congress. Because the legislative branch was (and continues to be) generally more susceptible to political pressures from domestic industries, congressional ascendancy served to perpetuate high tariff protection. It also consigned the executive branch to a peripheral role in nineteenth century trade policy. Negotiations were hindered not only by congressional reluctance to cede power to the president, but also by a stubborn U.S. adherence to the principle of conditional most-favored-nation treatment. The conditional MFN principle required

Table 1–1
U.S. Tariff Rates. 1789–1984
(*in $ millions and percentages*)

	Imports	Percent Duty-Free	Calculated Duties	Ratio of Calculated Duties to		
				Total Imports	Dutiable Imports	Federal Revenue
1984	322,990	31.9	12,042	3.7	5.5	1.4
1980	244,007	43.8	7,535	3.1	5.7	1.4
1975	96,516	32.2	3,780	3.9	5.8	1.3
1970	39,756	34.9	2,584	6.5	9.9	1.2
1965	21,283	34.9	1,643	7.7	11.9	1.2
1960	14,650	39.5	1,084	7.4	12.2	1.2
1955	11,337	53.3	633	5.6	12.0	0.9
1950	8,743	54.5	522	6.0	13.1	1.0
1945	4,098	67.1	381	9.3	28.2	0.7
1940	2,541	64.9	318	12.5	35.6	5.9
1935	2,039	59.1	357	17.5	42.9	9.0
1932	1,325	66.9	260	19.6	59.1	16.3
1930	3,114	66.8	462	14.8	44.7	14.1
1925	4,176	64.9	552	13.2	37.6	14.5
1920	5,102	61.1	326	6.4	16.4	4.8
1915	1,648	49.2	206	12.5	33.5	30.1
1910	1,547	49.2	327	21.1	41.6	49.4
1900	831	44.2	229	27.6	49.5	41.1
1890	766	33.7	227	29.6	44.6	57.0
1880	628	33.1	183	29.1	43.5	55.9
1870	426	4.7	192	44.9	47.1	47.3
1860	336	20.2	53	15.7	19.7	94.9
1850	164	9.8	40	24.5	27.1	91.0
1840	86	48.8	15	17.6	34.4	69.3
1830	50	8.0	28	57.3	61.7	88.2
1820	74	n.a.	15	20.3	n.a.	83.9
1810	85	n.a.	9	10.6	n.a.	91.5
1800	91	n.a.	9	9.9	n.a.	83.7
1789–1791	n.a.	n.a.	4	n.a.	n.a.	99.5

Source: Adapted from Bureau of the Census, *Historical Statistics of the United States, Colonial Times to 1957; Statistical Abstract of the United States* (various editions).

Note: The ratios shown were calculated by the Bureau of the Census on the basis of figures quoted in thousands rather than millions of dollars.

n.a. = not available.

that each new trade pact be negotiated from scratch. Few trade agreements were reached during this period, and fewer still were ratified by the Senate.

During the Progressive era of the early twentieth century, opponents of protectionism slowly gained ground over the status quo. Diverse interest groups attacked the protectionist underpinnings of the tariff, arguing in turn that it stifled exports, strengthened the "trusts" at the expense of the workingman, limited consumer choice, and inhibited industrial progress. Free traders in the academic community made common cause with reform politicians and export industries to argue for liberal trade. The watchword of the day was to "take politics out of the tariff" by strengthening the negotiating powers of the executive branch, and by establishing a nonpartisan tariff commission to advise the executive and legislative branches. These proposals were resisted on Capitol Hill, which obviously stood to lose a great deal of power if the initiatives were adopted. A few fitful experiments with tariff commissions in the late nineteenth and early twentieth centuries failed, largely because they were partisan creations that lacked political credibility.

Tariff reform became more palatable for the U.S. Treasury in 1913, when the institution of the income tax created an alternative to continued dependence on import duties. The same legislation that created a national income tax also enacted the first significant reductions in the tariff since the Civil War. Four years later, Congress established an independent U.S. Tariff Commission as an advisory agency to both the executive and legislative branches.[2] Although the commission had no authority to set tariffs or unilaterally alter the course of U.S. policy, its creation was an important step in the move toward a "scientific" (that is, nonpolitical) tariff policy.

The Congress remained in control of the tariff, however, as it demonstrated in 1922 by restoring duties to protective levels. The most dramatic reassertion of congressional authority came in 1930, when the infamous Smoot–Hawley Tariff raised the average tariff rate on dutiable products to its highest level in U.S. history. Following on the heels of the crash of 1929, U.S. trading partners reacted to the Smoot–Hawley Tariff by erecting retaliatory trade barriers.

The New Deal marked a watershed in the internationalization of U.S. trade policy. Secretary of State Cordell Hull built upon the efforts of his predecessor, Charles Evans Hughes, to make the unconditional most-favored nation (MFN) principle the new foundation of U.S. trade policy. The unconditional MFN obliges the automatic extension of tariff reductions or other privileges given to one nation to all other nations that pledge and receive reciprocal MFN treatment. Hull hoped that by negotiating a series of bilateral trade agreements incorporating the MFN principle, the United States would create a network of interlocking agreements that would restore the world to a more liberal trading system.

The Congress granted the executive branch the negotiating authority it needed in the Reciprocal Trade Agreements Act of 1934. This historic legislation essentially reversed the balance of power between the executive and legislative branches by allowing the president to negotiate tariff-reduction agreements that did not require congressional ratification. The Congress did not relinquish all control over trade relations, however. The 1934 Act—and all subsequent grants of authority—limited the duration and degree of the president's tariff-cutting power. The act restricted the amount of such reductions to no more than 50 percent of existing rates, and initially provided the authority for only three years.

Franklin D. Roosevelt's administration negotiated reciprocity agreements with seven countries over the next two years, and the Congress subsequently renewed the authority eleven times over the next three decades. The agreements negotiated prior to World War II had the practical effect of nullifying the Smoot–Hawley tariff hikes. As can be seen in table 1–1, the average tariff on dutiable goods was 44.7 percent in 1930, and rose to a high-water mark of 59.1 percent by 1932, but fell to 35.6 percent by 1940. These average figures mask the benefits that accrued to the countries that reached reciprocity agreements with the United States. The duties they paid were well below those applied to other countries, and with each passing year, it became more attractive for new countries to negotiate themselves into the "MFN Club." These negotiations continued right through the Second World War; by the middle of that conflagration, the United States had concluded thirty bilateral agreements with twenty-five countries.

When the war ended in 1945, the United States emerged as the unchallenged political and economic leader of the western world. Washington used this opportunity to sponsor the creation of a more comprehensive and liberal international trading system based on a multilateral application of the unconditional MFN principle. The U.S. goal was to establish an International Trade Organization (ITO), along the same lines as the International Monetary Fund and the International Bank for Reconstruction and Development (the World Bank). These three institutions were to form the foundation of the postwar Bretton Woods economic system, in which supranational organizations would help to guide their member states in pursuing mutually advantageous economic relations. The United States viewed this not simply as an alluring economic prospect, but also as the surest guarantee of postwar peace, stability, and prosperity. The strategic political importance of a liberal trade policy tended to mute the objections raised at a tactical political level. The bipartisan support for executive initiatives during the Cold War discouraged the Congress from derailing liberal trade.

The countries that drafted the ITO's charter in 1946 also created a provisional General Agreement on Tariffs and Trade (GATT) that would govern their trade relations until the ITO was fully ratified. The 1945 extension of the Reciprocal Trade Agreements Act provided the authority for the United States to join the provisional GATT without formal Senate ratification of the Agreement.[3] The grand expectations of the ITO seemed dashed by the refusal of the U.S. Senate to ratify the organization's charter, but the GATT then stepped in as the ITO's institutional understudy. The GATT was never intended to function as a permanent institution, but by historical accident it evolved into the de facto centerpiece of the international trading system. Starting with twenty-three contracting parties in 1947, by 1984 the "temporary" organization encompassed 121 countries that collectively accounted for the bulk of world trade.[4] During the four decades since its founding, the GATT has created an evolving body of international trade law, provided a forum for settling disputes among its signatories, and served as the venue for seven rounds of multilateral trade negotiations (MTNs) that have brought tariffs down to a fraction of their prewar levels.

While the GATT shares responsibility for the remarkable progress made in postwar trade expansion, it has sometimes been hard-pressed to keep up with the creativity shown by its member states in devising new and innovative means to restrict foreign competition. The decline of tariffs as an instrument of protection has given rise to nontariff barriers (NTBs) such as unilateral quotas, prohibitive product standards, abuses in the trade-remedy laws, interventionist foreign investment regimes, and restrictive agreements providing for "voluntary" export restraints and "orderly marketing arrangements." The GATT has a mixed record in its efforts to bring NTBs under control.

The first five rounds of multilateral trade negotiations in the GATT dealt almost exclusively with tariffs. The first serious consideration of nontariff barriers came during the Kennedy Round (1964–1967), when the contracting parties negotiated an Antidumping Code. By the time of the Tokyo Round (1973–1979), tariffs in the industrialized countries had been cut so deeply that NTBs took center stage. Negotiators redrafted the Antidumping Code, which had failed to be ratified by the U.S. Senate, and drew up nearly a dozen other agreements dealing with subsidies, government procurement policies, trade in beef and dairy products, import licensing procedures, and other matters. All of these issues went beyond the relatively technical and quantifiable concerns of tariffs, and touched upon more sensitive questions of each government's economic policies.

Because consensus among the GATT nations proved elusive in these issues, the negotiators decided to allow each nation to choose whether or not to adhere to the new agreements. Rather than fold these codes into the GATT through amendment and ratification of the General Agreement itself, the principle of "code reciprocity" was established. The codes would be treated as separate agreements with their own rules and dispute-settlement mechanisms, and many of the rights and obligations conferred by the agreements would be restricted to those countries that ratified them. Since the conclusion of the Tokyo Round in 1979, most of the industrialized signatories to the GATT have adopted the codes, but only a handful of the developing countries have ratified them. Some observers have criticized this development as a "Balkanization of international trade policy," while others believe that progress in trade liberalization should not be retarded by an attempt to satisfy the lowest common denominator in each nation's trade policies.[5]

The GATT's effectiveness is further diminished by the divisions among its members over several fundamental issues, such as the question of how developing countries should be incorporated in the international trading system. While signatories agree in principle that developing countries should be accorded special and differential treatment, they remain sharply divided over the precise form that this treatment is to take. Developing countries question the relevance of an organization that allows self-perpetuating and discriminatory exceptions for trade in agricultural products and textiles. Another perennial problem within the GATT is the inadequacy of the dispute-settlement procedures, which remain open to dilatory maneuvers and procedural squabbles.

These shortcomings notwithstanding, the GATT continues to perform its central function of providing a relatively stable framework for trade among its signatories. Compared with the United Nations Security Council or the International Court of Justice, the GATT has been relatively successful in lending discipline to its area of competence. Disputes may flare up between the United States and the other parties to the agreement, but the GATT provides them with the guidelines and good offices to resolve these problems—or at least to smooth out the rough edges. By the same token, it is axiomatic that this means restraining some of the freedom of movement previously enjoyed by the United States and other GATT members.

U.S. Trade Policy within the GATT System

The success of U.S.-sponsored trade liberalization is shown by the tremendous growth in trade since World War II, with the attendant gains in efficiency and employment. While economic liberalism teaches that expanded trade brings the greatest good for the greatest number by creating new export markets and rationalizing the international division of labor, trade also forces declining industries to face the pain of adjustment. Domestic industries that are challenged by international competition frequently demand relief, but the GATT strictly limits the scope for such exceptions. The commitments made in the GATT mean that the U.S. market could not be as easily closed in 1984 as it could be in 1884, when raising the tariff was a comparatively simple matter of domestic policy.

Under the GATT system, protection is—at least ideally—a controlled exception to the rule of liberal trade. When the United States wishes to impose a new trade barrier, it must do so in a limited and justified fashion, with transparent and predictable bureaucratic procedures. The various domestic trade-remedy laws and GATT rules allow the member countries to take action against competitors who engage in unfair trade practices, or to temporarily impose import relief when unforeseen circumstances arise. The trade-remedy statutes replace the outright protectionism of the nineteenth century with a quasi-judicial system under which the party seeking restrictions must prove its case on factual grounds. Any deviation from the GATT norms requires that compensation be given to the countries whose exports are affected; if no compensation is granted, then GATT rules allow the other members of the system to retaliate against the offending party.

Beleaguered industries look to the trade-remedy laws as their first line of defense, but they sometimes turn to the Congress as their court of last resort. The Congress is usually more receptive to these demands than is the executive branch, and disputes over import relief often upset the delicate balance between the executive and legislative branches. If the trade-remedy laws do not stem imports, then the industries may press for specific acts of import relief, such as higher tariffs or import quotas, or ask the Congress to change the U.S. trade-remedy laws to make the statutes work in their favor.

Conflict between the internationalists in the executive branch and advocates of special interests in the Congress grew especially intense during the early 1980s, when the U.S. trade deficit rose to unprecedented heights. The merchandise balance had been in the red throughout the 1970s, but never broke the $40 billion barrier during that decade. The deficit climbed steadily from $28.1 billion in 1981 to $36.4 billion in 1982, $60.1 billion in 1983, and a record $123.3 billion in 1984. The merchandise trade deficit caused the current account to plummet, and the steady capital outflow made the United States a net debtor by mid-1985—a position it had not held since World War I. When combined with the recession of 1982–1983, the first half of the decade was a difficult time for the advocates of liberal trade policies. The sheer number of legislative proposals relating to trade might be taken as a crude index of congressional interest and the politicization of the issue. The 98th Congress witnessed the introduction of 882 bills and resolutions pertaining to foreign trade, versus 249 such proposals considered by the 93rd Congress a decade earlier.[6]

The burgeoning deficit was attributed to several causes, including heightened demand when the U.S. economic recovery outstripped that of its trading partners in 1983–1984, an overvalued dollar, and declining productivity in several U.S. industries, but many members of Congress also viewed the deficit as a product of misguided U.S. trade policy. Ever since the passage of the Reciprocal Trade Agreements Act of 1934, the congressional majority in favor of liberal trade has been opposed by a dissenting minority fighting a rearguard action. For most of the last half century, these critics have lacked the power to enact their own legislative program, such as the Burke–Hartke quota bill of 1971, but have had sufficient strength to block, delay, or weaken several liberal trade initiatives. The dissenters blocked Senate ratification of the International Trade Organization (ITO) charter, and President Nixon's proposals for trade legislation in 1969 and 1973 were held up until the passage of the Trade Act of 1974.

During the 97th and 98th Congresses, however, the opponents of liberal trade grew in numbers and influence. The members of this clique tended to be urban more often than rural, Democrats more often than Republicans, and members of the House more often than senators, but the chief characteristic they shared was a significant number of constituents who appeared to have suffered from increased import competition.[7] Mature industries such as steel, textiles, footwear, and automobiles comprised the hard core of this faction, and its political center of gravity rested in the House Committee on Energy and Commerce. Although the Ways and Means Committee has principal jurisdiction over trade policy in the House—a holdover from the days when the tariff was primarily a revenue instrument—the Energy and Commerce Committee challenged their preeminence.

The central tenet of the Energy and Commerce Committee and its coreligionists was that liberal trade cannot succeed if only one country adheres to its principles. In view of the many tariff and nontariff restrictions imposed by U.S. trading partners, the committee argued that:

> The current U.S. approach—concentrating entirely on advocating and promoting a world-wide system of "free trade"—is unrealistic and, given the inherent theoretical and practical limitations to free trade, not necessarily in the best interest of the United States. Instead, U.S. policy should look beyond simply promoting "free trade" toward a set of specific national goals to be pursued in the international arena.[8]

Among the specific national goals that the committee advocated were the negotiation of "international agreements to rationalize world trade in commodities" modeled after the Multi Fiber Arrangement that tightly controls trade in textiles and apparel, or the establishment of unilateral limitations on certain imports. Several proposals were floated during the 97th and 98th Congresses to negotiate quotas or impose unilateral restrictions on copper, steel, footwear, and other products. The Energy and Commerce Committee also reported out legislation that would require that automobiles contain a minimum domestic content. This bill passed the House in 1983, but stalled in the Senate.

While most members of Congress would not go as far the Energy and Commerce Committee wished, and the Ways and Means Committee maintained its position as the preeminent trade voice in the House, the weight of congressional opinion began to shift toward a more restrictive trade policy. As an alternative to outright market protection, some members advocated a reciprocity policy based on the belief that the U.S. market is far more open than the global norm. The new goal for U.S. trade negotiators would be to pressure foreign governments into lowering their barriers on specific products down to the levels imposed by the United States on the same goods, or else the U.S. barriers would be raised in retaliation. Although this approach to reciprocity had the appeal of appearing superficially fair, critics charged that it would mean abandoning the GATT principles of comparative advantage and unconditional most-favored-nation treatment. They claimed it would also invite counter-retaliation and threaten to undo the progress made in the past seven rounds of multilateral trade negotiations.

The Reagan administration rejected the "if you can't beat 'em, join 'em" methods of dealing with foreign transgressions. The 1981 white paper on U.S. trade policy declared that "we will strongly resist protectionist pressure,"[9] and argued that the proper answer to foreign restrictions is to strengthen the liberal trading system rather than to respond in kind. The administration pledged that it would strictly enforce U.S. laws and international agreements; it also wanted the Congress to grant it the negotiating authority needed to convince U.S. trading partners to open their own markets. The Reagan administration's goals in these negotiations would go beyond traditional concerns such as agricultural exports and improving the dispute-settlement procedures of the GATT, and would include new issues such as trade in services and high technology products, trade-related investment, and intellectual property rights. The White House also hoped to renew the Generalized System of Preferences (GSP), a program that offers tariff preferences for developing countries, and to use the renewed GSP in negotiations with its beneficiary developing countries.

Despite its rhetoric, the Reagan administration's commitment to liberal trade was far from absolute during its first term. The White House consistently opposed protectionist initiatives in the Congress, and was instrumental in determining the content of the Trade and Tariff Act of 1984, but did not resist all temptations to restrict imports through executive action. The administration took a hard line against textile imports by negotiating strict bilateral agreements with several developing countries. Japanese automobile imports were restricted through a "temporary" voluntary restraint agreement with Tokyo in 1981, which was then extended in each of the next three years. The president also agreed to provide import relief under the escape clause for motorcycles and specialty steel products, while a relief petition from the carbon steel industry was rewarded with an import relief plan that was technically outside of the escape-clause provisions. In most instances, the administration argued that these concessions to protectionist sentiment were pragmatic compromises that forestalled the passage of even tighter restrictions by the Congress.[10]

The Reagan administration's pragmatism did not placate its critics on Capitol Hill. Conflict over these issues kept trade legislation in a stalemate for nearly four years. The only significant trade legislation passed between 1981 and late 1984 was the one-way free trade area of the president's Caribbean Basin Initiative, which the Congress only reluctantly enacted in 1983.[11]

The stalemate was broken in the closing weeks of the 98th Congress, when the Reagan administration pushed hard for two programs that enjoyed wide support in the Congress. The first was the authority to conclude negotiations for a free trade agreement with Israel and to submit the agreement to the Congress on an expedited fast track for ratification. The second proposal would allow the president to pursue his import relief program for the carbon steel industry. The momentum in favor of these two programs led the Senate to transform what had been a simple tariff bill (H.R. 3398) into an omnibus package. Both houses then passed a wide range of measures in a series of eleventh-hour votes. Legislators and lobbyists scrambled to have their bills included in the burgeoning trade package, and the administration also took advantage of the opportunity to urge passage of less popular initiatives such as renewal of the GSP.

The House and the Senate passed all of the administration's priority bills, together with several of the restrictive measures that the White House opposed. The Senate bill was particularly objectionable from the liberal trader's point of view. The differences between the House and Senate bills were worked out in a conference committee, with administration representatives using this last opportunity to urge that the more blatantly restrictive provisions be dropped. A presidential veto was threatened if the final package was too heavily weighted toward protectionism. The passage of the TTA was made possible by the willingness of the conferees to delete or soften most of the provisions that the administration opposed. The president signed the bill into law on October 30, 1984.

Considering the frenetic pace of the closing hours of the 98th Congress, it is not surprising that the TTA became, in the parlance of Capitol Hill, a "Christmas tree" on which numerous legislative ornaments were hung. What is surprising is the relatively liberal or neutral character of the final package. Despite the pressures of the trade deficit and an impending presidential election, the Reagan administration and liberal trade advocates won many more battles than they lost. This is largely attributable to the bipartisan cooperation of the congressional trade committee leadership as well as coordination with the administration's representatives. The only major outbreaks of restrictive amendments came when the bill was considered on the floor of the Senate. The members of the Senate Finance Committee temporarily lost control of the legislation, but the conference committee was able to defeat most of the floor amendments.

Overview of the TTA

The Trade and Tariff Act of 1984's provisions may be divided into three broad areas: authority for the executive branch to negotiate with and (in some instances) retaliate against U.S. trading partners, the operation of the trade-remedy laws, and measures that relate to specific products. These provisions are described next.

Negotiating Objectives and Authority

The executive and legislative branches share concurrent power in foreign policy, with the constitutional ambiguities in this relationship often termed an invitation to struggle. The Congress wishes to retain its prerogatives in trade policy, but generally recognizes that the executive branch cannot be kept on a short leash if it wishes to obtain U.S. objectives. Over the course of the past two hundred years, three separate mechanisms have been developed to allow for varying degrees of congressional participation in trade diplomacy: ratification of treaties, limited grants allowing the president to reach executive agreements that do not require ratification, and expedited congressional approval of certain types of agreements.

The Constitution clearly provides a right of congressional participation in foreign policy by requiring Senate ratification of any treaty. Until the early twentieth century, this was virtually the only means by which the Congress would allow the executive branch to negotiate with U.S. trading partners. It proved to be an unwieldy device. Ratification is a take-it-or-leave-it proposition, and if at least one-third of the Senate objects to the terms of a treaty, it is doomed to failure. The upper chamber vetoed all but a handful of the trade agreements negotiated during the nineteenth century, and later refused to ratify the charter of the International Trade Organization in 1947.

The Senate's authority to block trade agreements was considered to be an appropriate check on executive power as long as the United States followed a policy of high tariff protection and economic isolationism, but the wisdom of this policy came under question when the United States began to emerge as an economic and political power. If the executive branch was to negotiate trade liberalization agreements with foreign governments, it needed greater flexibility. One solution to this problem was to allow the president to reach executive agreements with foreign governments without requiring that these agreements be ratified by the Senate. The first such authority was granted by the Reciprocal Trade Agreements Act of 1934. Congress maintained some control, however, by limiting the degree and duration of the discretion granted in this and all subsequent tariff-negotiating authorities. The 1934 act allowed tariff cuts of no more than 50 percent, and was initially granted for just three years.

The most recent tariff-negotiating authorities have followed the pattern set in 1934. Under the Trade Act of 1974, the executive branch could negotiate agreements to reduce duties by up to 60 percent of existing rates, or down to zero duty if the existing rate was 5 percent or less. The full tariff-cutting authority only lasted from 1975 to 1980—the period of the Tokyo Round MTN—while some residual authority was in place through January 2, 1982. Since the expiration of the MTN negotiating authority, the executive branch had no explicit congressional mandate to reach tariff agreements that do not require congressional ratification.

The third option for congressional participation in trade negotiations follows a middle road between Senate ratification and the authority to reach executive agreements. In some instances, the Congress will allow the executive branch to negotiate agreements that require expedited ratification by both houses on a special fast track. The fast track is designed to move the implementing legislation for a trade agreement through the Senate Finance Committee, House Ways and Means Committee, and the respective floors of both houses under a ninety-day deadline and without any amendments. The purpose of this mechanism is to allow *ex post* congressional approval or disapproval of trade agreements, without requiring that two-thirds of the Senate approve or allowing amendments or reservations. (An authority to negotiate compensation agreements for restrictions imposed under the escape clause constitutes an additional bargaining power for the executive branch, but it is restricted to special circumstances.)[12]

The Reagan administration had only a limited scope for negotiations during its first term. The residual tariff-cutting authority that was granted in the 1974 act expired one year after President Reagan was inaugurated. The Trade Act of 1974 did allow for the negotiation and ratification of agreements on nontariff barriers (NTBs) along the fast track, but this authority was not used from 1981 to 1984. The only trade agreements negotiated and approved during this period were limited sectoral arrangements involving semiconductors and civil aviation products, both of which are ratified in sections of the TTA.[13]

The lack of explicit negotiating authority did not keep the Reagan administration from drawing up an ambitious agenda. In addition to pursuing established goals of tariff reduction, promotion of U.S. agricultural exports, reform in the GATT dispute-settlement procedures, and rationalization of the nontariff codes, the White House hoped to launch negotiation on new issues such as trade in services, trade-related investment issues, intellectual property rights, and trade in high technology goods. None of these issues are presently covered extensively by the GATT. The administration also hoped to put pressure on the more competitive developing nations—the newly industrialized countries (NICs) —to open their markets and reduce the role of state intervention in their economies.

The Reagan administration planned to pursue these goals in a new round of multilateral trade negotiations in the GATT, but made no effort in its first term to obtain explicit authority for such negotiations from the Congress. The administration's immediate task was to convince U.S. trading partners that a new round is desirable in the first place, which as of 1984 was still a difficult proposition. Rather than request new MTN authority from the Congress— which may have proven even harder to obtain than agreement with U.S. trading partners—the White House pursued much more modest goals on Capitol Hill. The executive branch sought the authority to negotiate a more rapid phase-in of the Tokyo Round tariff reductions, as well as renewal of the residual tariff authority that expired in 1982, but the Congress rejected even these fairly modest proposals.

The Congress endorsed the administration's goals in the new issues by establishing negotiating objectives in the TTA for each of these areas, but it granted only limited means for achieving these objectives. First, it strengthened the president's retaliatory authority granted in section 301 of the Trade Act of

1974. This statute allows the president to take "all appropriate and feasible action" to assure that U.S. rights under trade agreements are observed by foreign parties. Under the amendments made in the 1984 act, the section 301 authority may be used more aggressively and frequently. The statute may be used to persuade other governments to modify their policies in the areas covered by the new issues.

Although multilateral tariff authority is still beyond the reach of the executive branch, the Trade and Tariff Act provides the president with bilateral tariff authority. Title IV of the TTA specifically allows the president to negotiate a free trade area (FTA) with Israel and it arranges for expedited congressional procedures for the ratification of such an agreement. Unlike all other tariff authorities granted since 1934, however, the TTA stipulates that any reductions granted in such agreements will not be automatically extended to other countries that are entitled to unconditional most-favored-nation treatment. This authority was used in 1985 to ratify the U.S.–Israeli FTA, which by 1995 will eliminate all tariffs between the two countries.

The authority of this title can also be used to negotiate exclusive bilateral tariff agreements with other countries. In order to enter into such negotiations, the executive branch must first consult with the House Ways and Means Committee and the Senate Finance Committee. It is possible that this authority will be used to ratify agreements with Canada, Mexico, or the member countries of the Association of South East Asian Nations (ASEAN), but as of late 1985 there were no such negotiations underway yet.

The implications of a discriminatory negotiating authority are disturbing for free trade purists, who are concerned that bilateral or regional agreements weaken the nondiscriminatory and multilateral underpinnings of the GATT system. For its part, the Reagan administration prefers multilateral over bilateral negotiations.

A third negotiating potential in the TTA is embodied in the renewed Generalized System of Preferences (GSP). This decade-old program provides duty-free access to the U.S. market for many imports from developing countries, on the theory that trade is superior to aid in encouraging economic development. The GSP was due to expire in January 1985. Developing countries hoped that the renewal legislation would overcome the program's shortcomings, but substantive reforms were politically difficult during 1984. GSP renewal was opposed by the unions, and many industry groups requested that their products be excluded from its coverage.

The Congress renewed the program until mid-1993, and defeated attempts to remove certain products or countries from its coverage or otherwise undercut the program, but the Congress also made an important change in the nature of the GSP at the request of the administration. The program must maintain at least the appearance of nonreciprocity in order to remain consistent with the GATT, but the TTA introduces a new element of negotiability. This is done by subjecting GSP products from the more competitive beneficiary countries to easier graduation (removal from eligibility) and also by allowing the president to provide improved market access through a special waiver. Executive decisions to limit or expand GSP benefits will be based on part on the concessions made by beneficiary countries. This neoreciprocity will increase the U.S. Trade Representative's leverage in dealing with developing countries, especially the newly industrialized countries. The United States will be able to alternately entice or threaten these nations to liberalize their trade regimes, cooperate in anticounterfeiting plans, improve the observance of labor rights, provide greater access to U.S. investors, or otherwise meet the concerns of U.S. trade negotiators.

It is now in the power of the president to make the program more or less liberal than it presently is for any given country, depending on the stance taken by the administration and the outcome of negotiations. The new leverage should not be overestimated, however; it is limited by those very factors that have restricted the value of the GSP program, such as limited product coverage and low U.S. duty rates.

Trade-Remedy Laws

The United States employs a panoply of trade-remedy laws that collectively form a system of "contingent protection" for domestic industries; import relief can be provided, but only if certain conditions are first met. The statutes vary according to the areas of concern, the standards of injury that must be proven, the remedies that are available, the agencies that execute them, and the procedures that they follow. The chief characteristics of the most widely used laws are summarized on table 1–2.

The most comprehensive form of import relief is available through the so-called escape clause (section 201 of the Trade Act of 1974), under which the United States can temporarily restrict imports of a given product from all foreign sources. Unlike most other remedy laws, the escape clause does not require that the imports be unfairly traded in order to be restricted. The chief criterion is that increasing imports must be a "substantial cause" of "serious injury" to the domestic industry. If the U.S. International Trade Commission (USITC) finds that this is the case, it must recommend an appropriate form of import relief to the president.

The president has complete discretion to accept, reject, or modify this plan. The White House considers not only the facts presented by the USITC, but also political and economic arguments presented by other federal agencies. The president's decision rests on whether the national economic interest would be best served by granting or not granting relief. Should the president decide to restrict imports, then the affected U.S. trading partners have a right to seek compensation in the form of some other market liberalization. If the United States does not extend such compensation, then the affected countries may restrict a substantially equivalent amount of imports from the United States.

Table 1-2
Principal U.S. Trade-Remedy Laws

Statute	Focus	Criteria	Available Remedies	Administrative Authorities
Sec. 201 ("escape clause")	Injurious imports	Increasing imports are a substantial cause of serious injury	Duties Quotas Tariff-rate quotas Adjustment assistance Orderly marketing arrangements	USITC President[a]
Sec. 701	Subsidized imports	Material injury[b]	Countervailing duties	USITC ITA
Sec. 731	Dumping (selling at less than fair value)	Material injury	Antidumping duties	USITC ITA
Sec. 301	Violations of trade agreements and commitments	Actions are unreasonable, unjustified, or discriminatory	"All appropriate and feasible action"	USTR President
Sec. 337	Unfair trade practices (for example, trademark or patent infringement)	Actions destroy or substantially injure an industry.	Exclusion orders Cease and desist orders	USITC President
Sec. 22	Agricultural imports below U.S. prices	Material interference with price-support programs	Import fees Quotas	USITC USDA President
Sec. 406	Disruptive imports from communist countries	Significant cause of material injury	Duties Quotas	USITC President

ITA: International Trade Administration of the U.S. Department of Commerce
USDA: U.S. Department of Agriculture
USITC: U.S. International Trade Commission
USTR: Office of the U.S. Trade Representative
[a]The Congress may override the president.
[b]The material injury test is only extended to countries that fulfill certain conditions.

Other trade-remedy laws do not require such compensation, provided that they are implemented in a manner consistent with GATT rules.

The antisubsidy and antidumping sections of the Tariff Act of 1930 deal with subsidized and dumped imports, respectively. If the International Trade Administration (ITA) of the Department of Commerce finds that an import is dumped (sold at less than fair value), and the USITC finds that this causes or threatens to cause material injury to the domestic industry, then antidumping duties (ADs) may be assessed against the imports. Countervailing duties (CVDs) may be ordered against imports that are found to benefit from subsidies. The USITC injury test is only extended in CVD cases when countries have met certain prior conditions or when it is otherwise required by U.S. international obligations.

Section 301 of the Trade Act of 1974 is a "presidential retaliation authority" under which private parties may petition the U.S. government to enforce U.S. trade rights. The statute provides the president with significant authority to retaliate against foreign trade practices, in order to give him leverage in negotiations. Because this statute is more a negotiating power than a trade-remedy law per se, it is discussed in greater detail in the negotiations section of this book.

Section 337 of the Tariff Act of 1930 gives the USITC the authority to restrict unfairly traded imports, such as counterfeit goods that infringe on registered patent or trademarks, if it can be shown that these imports may destroy or substantially injure a U.S. industry. The law allows the USITC to issue cease and desist orders or exclusion orders, the latter being the single most powerful sanction available under the trade-remedy statutes. The president may approve, disapprove, or fail to disapprove any USITC orders made under this authority.

Section 22 of the Agricultural Adjustment Act of 1933 allows the president to restrict imports that threaten material interference with domestic price support programs for farm products. The president generally takes temporary emergency action upon the recommendation of the Secretary of Agriculture, and then awaits the advice of the USITC for further action.

Under section 406 of the Trade Act of 1974, the United States can place duties or quotas on disruptive imports from communist countries. Due in part to the comparatively low level of east–west trade in the postdetente period, this law has been employed only ten times.

The various U.S. trade-remedy statutes are by no means mutually exclusive. The circumstances of an individual case may offer potential petitioners several possible choices among the laws. The decision to choose one remedy approach over another is guided by the industry's judgment of the comparative costs and benefits. Section 301 has the least formal standard of proof, but is subject to greater executive discretion than any other statute. The escape clause offers the most sweeping relief, but also imposes the highest standard of proof and a great degree of political uncertainty. The laws relating to unfair trade practices (dumping and subsidization) present less demanding standards, but require that the unfair trade practices and the remedies they offer may only offset the price effect of the practice rather than offset the injury that the practice is alleged to cause. Some industries resolve the dilemma by simultaneously filing for relief under two or more trade laws. They might also take ancillary actions, such as pursuing protectionist legislation and petitioning the USTR to remove a product from GSP eligibility. In this way, they hope to lay down a rolling barrage of trade actions on their foreign competitors.

Until the 1970s, the trade-remedy laws operated at the fringes of U.S. trade policy. When the trade balance began to turn from a surplus to a deficit, however, the caseload began to grow significantly. During fiscal years 1978 through 1981, the USITC conducted an average of 93 investigations per year; by

1982–1985, this figure had more than doubled to 219 cases.[14] (These figures do not include CVD cases that did not require an injury test, and therefore were considered only by the Department of Commerce.) The high water mark was reached in fiscal year was 1982, when U.S. steel companies filed 144 AD and CVD petitions with the USITC.[15] The total number of cases filed is not a clear indication of the protection that the statutes actually extend to U.S. producers. During the period of fiscal year 1982 through the first half of fiscal year 1985, petitioners were rewarded with an average of 22 relief orders for every 100 filings.[16] The total value of imports covered by the relief orders issued over this same period equalled $2.9 billion, or roughly 1 percent of total U.S. imports during 1984.

The rules of the trade-remedy laws are themselves a battlefield for the groups that advocate opposing views in trade policy. Some argue that the statutes have not kept up with new developments in the market interventions practiced by foreign governments, and that they should be strengthened to help achieve the proverbial level playing field. Some of the proposals floated in the 98th Congress would have extended the scope of U.S. trade-remedy laws to cover subsidized or dumped inputs used to manufacture finished products that are then exported to the United States, made preferential prices for energy and other natural resources a prohibited subsidy practice, and tightened the investigative procedures used in cases involving dumping by communist countries.[17] Other proposals would have tightened procedures and resulted in more numerous and harsher restrictions. Critics viewed these initiatives as a subtle form of protectionism that could make U.S. trade-remedy laws inconsistent with the GATT and could invite retaliation against U.S. exports.

The 98th Congress witnessed a full-fledged battle between the protectionists and perfectionists, but no clear victor emerged. Industries and unions banded together in umbrella organizations such as the Trade Reform Action Coalition (TRAC) in order to advocate tighter trade-remedy laws. They were opposed by such groups as the U.S. Chamber of Commerce, the American Association of Exporters and Importers, and Consumers for World Trade as well as by the trade associations of manufactured and agricultural producers. Both groups enlisted the aid of like-minded congressmen, while the Reagan administration and its allies on Capitol Hill sided with the liberal trade faction. The liberal trade supporters ultimately succeeded in defeating most of the proposals that they opposed.

The escape-clause legislation came under close scrutiny by the 98th Congress, but was not drastically changed. The TTA amends the criteria for finding serious injury, and clarifies the mechanism under which the Congress can override presidential decisions. These amendments are not expected to have a major impact on the operation of the statute.

The changes in the AD and CVD statutes are far more extensive. Only a few measures will have a significant impact, but their net effect appears to favor petitioners over respondents. One requires the USITC to cumulate the imports from several suppliers in certain cases when making an injury finding. This provision will make it easier for the commission to find that imports from small suppliers cause or threaten to cause material injury to domestic industries, and will encourage petitioners to pad their petitions. Another amendment codifies and tightens the application of an existing investigative practice known as *upstream subsidization*. Under this approach, finished goods that contain subsidized inputs can be subject to countervailing duties, whether or not the goods themselves have been subsidized. Other amendments facilitate self-initiation of AD proceedings by the ITA in cases of "persistent dumping," lengthen the period during which a respondent may be found liable for retroactive duties, and place the burden of persuasion on the party that seeks revocation of an anti-dumping order in annual reviews. A few amendments aid respondents by eliminating the right of petitioners to appeal preliminary decisions and by lowering the level of the possible dumping margin (the dumping margin being the difference between an item's fair value and its price in the United States).

Other amendments might assist petitioners, respondents, and the administering agencies by easing the procedural burdens that the statutes impose. These reforms include expedited revocation of ADs and CVDs in cases where neither party shows any continued interest, and reduction of costly verification and review procedures. Still other modifications serve to codify existing procedures, and are intended to avoid any future court challenges based on claims that the USITC or the ITA went beyond their statutory authority.

The TTA does not lay to rest all controversies surrounding the trade-remedy laws. The groups that were rebuffed during the 98th Congress introduced old and new initiatives in the 99th. The debate will continue to center on such key considerations as the degree of executive discretion in the statutes, the injury criteria, who may file petitions, and the scope of foreign practices coming within their purview. The extent, duration, and timeliness of trade remedies will also remain a subject of dispute.

Measures Relating to Specific Products

Special protection or dispensation from the rules of the liberal trading system are occasionally made for certain products. The GATT system itself countenances a restrictive special import regime. The Multi Fiber Arrangement (MFA) and its predecessor agreements have established a "temporary" exception to the GATT rules since the early 1960s. The MFA and the many bilateral agreements negotiated under its auspices serve to restrict the access that developing countries enjoy to the markets of industrialized countries such as the United States.

Many countries unilaterally employ special import regimes for agricultural products, which are also allowed exceptional treatment under the GATT. Perhaps the most restrictive of all such regimes is the Common Agricultural

Program (CAP) of the European Community, which is a source of constant irritation for the United States and other major agricultural exporters. For its own part, the United States tightly restricts imports of sugar, dairy products, and other agricultural goods. The United States has had a special GATT waiver for these policies since 1955.

Mature or uncompetitive industries often request that they be granted exceptions to the rules of liberal trade above and beyond the relief offered by the escape clause. With the exceptions just noted, the United States generally resists the temptation to satisfy these demands. Any such deviations from obligations in the GATT must be paid for with compensation to the trading partners that are affected. Despite pressures from a wide range of special interests, the 98th Congress rejected nearly all of the quota bills and other restrictive initiatives that were floated for copper, footwear, and other products.

The single most significant departure from this general trend against product-specific measures is the Steel Import Stabilization Act of 1984 (title VIII of the TTA). This enacts the president's five-year relief program for the steel industry by granting the executive branch the power to enforce "voluntary" steel-export-restraint agreements. The act is less restrictive than the legislation proposed by the U.S. steel industry, but includes industrial policy provisions that were not part of the president's plan. The law stipulates that the steel industry must devote nearly all of its net cash flow to reinvestment and worker retraining, or else the government will no longer enforce the steel-import limitations.

Some tariff changes are also enacted by the TTA. Most U.S. duties are subject to binding maximum rates that were agreed to in one or more of the seven MTN rounds held under the auspices of the GATT. If duties are increased above these so called bindings without granting some form of compensation to the affected trading partners, then the other GATT members may retaliate against the United States. Although the Congress effectively transferred primary control over the Tariff Schedules of the United States (TSUS) to the trade negotiators in the executive branch in 1934, nearly all trade legislation still includes provisions that enact temporary or permanent modifications in the TSUS. These amendments may increase, decrease, suspend, or eliminate the rates of duty charged for any given item on the schedules, or reclassify the nomenclature.

During the 98th Congress, the Trade Subcommittee of the House Ways and Means Committee considered several dozen separate bills to amend the TSUS. The subcommittee heard testimony from 162 witnesses, making this somewhat atavistic practice the single most time-consuming order of business for the subcommittee. The proposals that passed this gauntlet were melded into the miscellaneous tariff bill (H.R. 3398) that ultimately became the vehicle for the Trade and Tariff Act of 1984. Titles I and II of the TTA make temporary and permanent changes in the tariff rates and classifications of dozens of items, ranging from the commonplace (for example, clock radios) to the obscure, such as 4,4′-Bis(a,a-dimethylbenzyl) diphenylamine. For the most part, the TSUS modifications made by the Congress are for comparatively minor and noncontroversial products, and the duty suspensions, reductions, and eliminations far outnumber the increases.

Other product-specific measures in the act include a nonbinding resolution expressing the sense of the Congress that the president should negotiate export controls with copper-producing countries, and a section denying favorable duty status for bicycle parts imported into the customs territory of the United States from foreign trade zones. The TTA also deals with the duties and responsibilities of the U.S. Customs Service and customhouse brokers, and establishes numerous customs rules relating to such matters as the importation of curios and relics, and the tariff implications of "importing" articles that return to the earth from outer space.

Notes

1. See John M. Dobson, *Two Centuries of Tariffs: The Background and Emergence of the U.S. International Trade Commission* (Washington, D.C.: U.S. Government Printing Office, 1976), appendix D, for a list of the major tariff and trade legislation from 1789 through 1974. The most important sections of the TTA amend the two pillars of U.S. trade law: the Tariff Act of 1930 and the Trade Act of 1974. The 1930 act (as amended) continues to provide the basic antidumping and countervailing duty statutes, together with several other trade-remedy provisions. The 1974 act (as amended) provides the authority for import relief under the escape clause (section 201) and the presidential retaliation statute (section 301), as well as negotiating powers (now mostly defunct) and the implementing legislation of the Generalized System of Preferences. Both the 1930 and 1974 acts were amended by the Trade Agreements Act of 1979.

2. See Dobson, *op. cit.*, for a history of the U.S. International Trade Commission and its predecessor agencies.

3. The U.S. Congress never formally ratified U.S. membership in the GATT, although the body of trade legislation passed since 1947 implicitly accepts the tenets of the GATT system.

4. See General Agreement on Tariffs and Trade, *International Trade* (Geneva, annual), *passim.*

5. R. Michael Gadbaw, "The Outlook for GATT as an Institution," in Seymour J. Rubin and Thomas R. Graham, eds., *Managing Trade Relations in the 1980s; Issues Involved in the GATT Ministerial Meeting of 1982* (Totowa, N.J.: Rowman & Allanheld, 1983), pp. 38–39.

6. See Michael R. Czinkota and Paul J. Kollmer, "Foreign Trade and the 98th Congress; Republicans and Democrats," Special Publication No.7 (Washington, D.C.: National Center for Export–Import Studies, 1984) (mimeo), p. 1.

7. *Ibid., passim.*

8. U.S. House of Representatives, Committee on Energy and Commerce, *The United States in a Changing World Economy: The Case for an Integrated Domestic and International Commercial Policy*, 98th Congress, 1st Session, Committee Print 98–N (1983).

9. See testimony of Ambassador William Brock, in U.S. Senate, Committee on Banking, Housing and Urban Affairs, *Oversight of U.S. Trade Policy*, Part 1, 97th Congress, 1st session, Hearing 97–39 (July 8 and 9, 1981), pp. 21–25.

10. See Stephen L. Lande and Craig VanGrasstek, "Trade with the Developing Countries: The Reagan Record and Prospects," in John W. Sewell et al., *U.S. Foreign Policy and the Third World: Agenda 1985–86*, U.S. Third World Policy Perspectives No. 3 (Washington, D.C.: Overseas Development Council, 1985).

11. See Permanent Secretariat of the Latin American Economic System, *The Caribbean Basin Initiative: An Evaluation of First-Year Results*, Document SP/CL/XI.O/DT No. 11 (Caracas, Venezuela: September 1985).

12. See chapter 5.

13. See chapter 2 on semiconductors and chapter 7 on civil aviation products.

14. Information supplied by the Office of Public and Consumer Affairs, U.S. International Trade Commission.

15. See Seeley G. Lodwick, "ITC Official Reveals Data on 'Unfair Trade' Cases," *The Journal of Commerce*, May 21, 1985.

16. *Ibid.*

17. For descriptions of these proposals, see the notes to chapter 6.

Part I
Negotiating Objectives and Authority

2
U.S. Negotiating Objectives: Reciprocity and Retaliation

The International Trade and Investment Act of 1984 (title III of the TTA) establishes U.S. negotiating objectives in several new issues that have not previously been the subject of full-scale international concern. The only specific tariff-negotiating authority granted by title III is limited to certain high technology products. The principal instrument offered by title III for achieving its objectives are direct consultations with foreign governments, backed up by resort to dispute-settlement proceedings and the presidential retaliatory authority offered by section 301 of the Trade Act of 1974 (as amended). Under this authority, the president can restrict access to the U.S. market for the products and services of other countries that engage in unreasonable, unjustifiable, or discriminatory trade practices. Title III also mandates certain additional activities, such as intergovernmental consultations and research on barriers to service exports.

The New Issues

A 1981 Reagan administration white paper laid out U.S. trade policy goals for the coming years.[1] The white paper formally introduced several new issues for international negotiations, including trade in services, trade-related investment, and high technology products. These subjects exist in a tabula rasa of little or no international rules, not having been comprehensively addressed by the GATT or other supranational institutions. In response to the growing complaints from U.S. corporations that their patents, trademarks, and copyrights are being violated by foreign pirates and counterfeiters, the issue of intellectual property rights was later added to the litany of new issues.

The Congress was quite receptive to the administration's emphasis on these new issues, but an extended dispute over the means for addressing them prevented Capitol Hill from giving its formal approval until passage of the TTA. Title III sets out U.S. negotiating objectives in each of these issues, and brings some of them explicitly within the scope of the presidential retaliation authority (section 301). The new issues are also dealt with in the bilateral negotiating authority (see chapter 3), the renewal of the Generalized System of Preferences (see chapter 4), and in some measures relating to specific products and issues (see chapter 7).

Services

Trade in services such as banking, transportation, construction, and insurance is among the least disciplined aspects of international economic relations, despite the fact that services account for an estimated 20 percent or more of all world trade.[2] The United States has a particularly deep interest in the services trade, given its heretofore unambiguous competitive advantage in this area. The domestic U.S. economy is dominated by services, which account for about two-thirds of the gross national product and about three-quarters of all private employment.[3] Services rank among the more promising sectors for export development. Some of the most competitive U.S. industries are in the fields of telecommunications, data processing and information management, engineering, and construction. Services are also significant because of their intimate connection with high technology industries and the export of capital goods.

The importance of services in U.S. international trade is readily shown by the statistics in table 2–1. Services accounted for about 40 percent of all exports from 1981 to 1984. In stark contrast to the chronic deficit in merchandise trade, the U.S. balance in services has been consistently in the black. While the surplus in the service sector offset the merchandise trade deficit in 1981, climbing service imports since then have cut the sectoral surplus in half. If these trends continue, the United States could soon become a net service importer.

Table 2–1
U.S. Trade Balances in Goods and Services
(balance of payments basis, in $ millions)

	1981	1982	1983	1984
Goods				
Exports	237,085	211,198	200,257	220,316
Imports	265,086	247,667	261,312	328,597
Balance	– 28,001	– 36,469	– 61,055	–108,281
Services				
Exports	138,637	138,252	131,945	142,105
Imports	97,508	102,923	103,802	123,944
Balance	41,129	35,329	28,143	18,161
Total	13,128	– 1,140	– 32,912	– 90,120

Source: Adapted from U.S. Department of Commerce, *Business America*, v. 8, no. 14 (July 8, 1985), p. 19.

The Reagan administration makes services one of its top priorities in trade negotiations. Because services are not explicitly and comprehensively covered by the GATT, the field is wide open for discussion. The only GATT code dealing with services in any way is the Agreement on Government Procurement, which exhorts its signatories to "consider" developing rules for trade in services. The Organization for Economic Cooperation and Development's (OECD) Code for the Liberalization of Current Invisible Transactions and Code of Liberalization of Capital Movements only apply to the industrialized OECD countries, and are restricted by various reservations and derogations lodged by signatory nations. The OECD codes have no enforcement mechanisms. Other agreements deal with specific sectors such as civil aviation, broadcasting, and maritime shipping.

The absence of generic and universally accepted rules on services has left the issue largely to the discretion of national governments. In the United States, the general pattern is one of private enterprise regulated primarily by the individual states. Within the state regulatory environment, foreign service providers are generally accorded national treatment, meaning that they may compete on an equal footing with domestic firms.

By contrast, many governments exclude or tightly restrict investment and imports from foreign purveyors of services. The rationale behind restrictions often rests on the concern that vital services such as broadcasting and transportation must not be subject to interference or manipulation by foreign interests. (The United States also requires that broadcasting enterprises be owned by U.S. citizens.) Services are often under the control of government monopolies, and where private firms are allowed to compete, foreign companies may be excluded or subject to discrimination. Other restrictions range from traditional barriers such as tariffs and import-licensing requirements, to discriminatory government procurement policies and local-content rules. Foreign service industries sometimes subsidize or dump their exports in the U.S. market, or otherwise benefit from unfair trade practices.

The United States hopes to bring trade in services under the same type of discipline that governs merchandise trade under the GATT: unconditional most-favored-nation and national treatment, negotiated reductions in tariff and nontariff barriers, and progressive liberalization among all trading partners. Ideally, the United States would like to achieve these goals in a new round of GATT negotiations.

Most industrialized countries received the U.S. initiative favorably though cautiously, but many developing countries object to discussing an issue that raises such sensitive matters of sovereign control. To date, the United States has only succeeded in bringing the issue to the multilateral table. The GATT's progress on services has been confined to the preparation of national studies by several industrialized countries and preliminary discussions of what an international services agreement might entail.[4]

If a multilateral services agreement proves to be elusive, the United States might attempt to reach agreements through bilateral or "plurilateral" negotiations (that is, discussions involving several countries, but not all GATT signatories). The United States and Israel took a first step toward concluding a comprehensive bilateral services agreement in a nonbinding protocol to their bilateral free trade agreement (see chapter 3). This is the first international agreement to provide a framework for the full range of trade in services. U.S. negotiators hope that the principles incorporated in this accord will lead to a more substantive understanding between the two countries, and set a precedent for future agreements with other nations. Other multilateral forums such as the OECD could be used to negotiate agreements, although the United States clearly wishes that the GATT be the lead institution. The section 301 retaliatory authority discussed later in this chapter may enhance the leverage of U.S. negotiators in bilateral discussions and exert pressure for initiating multilateral talks.

Definition of Services. The field of services has rightly been termed an "amorphous concept" that includes "various activities that do not neatly fit together except that they are not manufactured and commodity goods."[5] Section 306(a) of the TTA attempts to correct the confusion by defining services as "economic activities whose outputs are other than tangible goods." Examples of these activities include (but are not limited to):

> banking, insurance, transportation, communications and data processing, retail and wholesale trade, advertising, accounting, construction, design, engineering, management consulting, real estate, professional services, entertainment, education, health care and tourism.

Negotiating Objectives in Services. Section 305 of the TTA makes it an object of U.S. trade negotiations "to reduce or to eliminate barriers to, or other distortions of, international trade in services... including barriers that deny national treatment and restrictions on the establishment and operation in such markets." The United States also wishes "to develop internationally agreed rules, including dispute settlement procedures" that "will reduce or eliminate such barriers or distortions and help ensure open international trade in services."

Trade-Related Investment

Despite the self-evident importance of investment in transnational economic relations, there are almost no internationally accepted rules to regulate the relations between foreign investors and host governments. The unratified charter of the International Trade Organization included articles relating to investment issues, but the GATT itself is silent on this matter. The OECD Code of

Liberalization of Capital Movements could form the basis of an agreement among industrialized nations, but it is hindered by the limitations of the code itself and the reservations of its individual signatories. Some of the forty-eight bilateral treaties of friendship, commerce, and navigation to which the United States subscribe cover investment issues in a general way, and the United States is currently negotiating bilateral investment treaties with several of its trading partners. The United States may also resort to direct pressure. Investment disputes with developing countries can lead to the suspension or withdrawal of foreign aid or certain trade preferences, as provided under the Foreign Assistance Act of 1961, the Caribbean Basin Economic Recovery Act, and the renewal legislation of the Generalized System of Preferences (see chapter 4).

In the absence of international agreements, investment disputes have been among the most contentious issues in the history of U.S. international economic policy. The more traditional U.S. complaints have involved foreign restrictions on the right of establishment (that is, outright bans on certain types of investment), failure to provide national treatment for foreign investors, restrictions on profit remittances to the home country, and uncompensated expropriation or appropriation of property owned by U.S. individuals or corporations. Investment problems have been compounded in recent years by a trend toward placing tight restrictions on the operations of U.S.-owned multinational corporations (MNCs). Developing countries frequently use investment restrictions in an attempt to improve their trade balances, generate foreign exchange, encourage higher levels of processing within the country, and foster the transfer of technology. One common approach is to set performance requirements, such as those that mandate a minimum local content for manufactured goods in terms of local materials, labor, or equity, or else establish minimum export levels or maximum import content for finished goods. Other investment restrictions include outright bans on foreign ownership in certain fields, required local capital participation, and the mandatory transfer of advanced technologies.

The Reagan administration's 1981 white paper on trade policy argued that investment restrictions "distort trade flows just as seriously as do tariffs and nontariff barriers,"[6] and that the issue should receive high priority in U.S. trade negotiations. The administration recognized that investment issues raise sensitive questions and are likely to encounter strong resistance from U.S. trade partners. Many developing countries are concerned that negotiations on investment rules would be an indirect assault on their sovereignty and industrial policies.

The issue has been clouded at times by pressure in the United States for instituting similar policies, such as automotive local-content legislation. Another complicating factor is the differing interests of U.S. firms in pursuing the investment issue. Companies that do not yet have overseas investments tend to give higher priority to the matter than those that are already established abroad, and who therefore might fear retaliation for tough U.S. positions. Some U.S.

corporations are concerned that if their government pushes too hard on this issue, investors from other countries will receive unofficial preferential treatment by host countries. Established MNCs are also concerned that if the United States retaliates against investment restrictions by limiting imports from the host countries, their overseas affiliates or investments could be hurt. Some companies hope to bring the full weight of the U.S. government to bear on the host country, while others are concerned that government-to-government negotiations would be too confrontational.

Negotiating Objectives. Section 305 of the TTA states that the chief U.S. negotiating objectives in investment issues are to reduce or eliminate "artificial or trade-distorting barriers to foreign direct investment, to expand the principle of national treatment, and to reduce unreasonable barriers to establishment." U.S. negotiators will also attempt to develop internationally agreed upon rules, including dispute-settlement procedures, that "will help to ensure a free flow of foreign direct investment" and "will reduce or eliminate the trade distortive effects of certain investment related measures."

Trade in High Technology Products

Computers, telecommunications equipment, semiconductors, and other high technology products are at the cutting edge of merchandise trade. It is axiomatic that if an industrialized country wishes to remain competitive in the production and export of goods, it must stay current with the most advanced industrial products and production processes. Keeping export markets open is also imperative. The United States is concerned not only with the competitive challenge posed by Japan (whose industrial progress has relied heavily on the development and exploitation of technological innovations), but also with the efforts of less advanced competitors to establish their own high technology industries.

Several European countries and some of the more sophisticated developing countries fear that the United States and Japan could form a de facto oligopoly in high technology products, which would relegate them to a perpetual second-class status in the world economy. Industrialized and developing countries alike have therefore instituted industrial-targeting and import-substitution policies in order to narrow the technological gap. These policies entail the use of high tariff and nontariff barriers to protect their infant industries, subsidized research and development, discriminatory government procurement practices, and restrictions on foreign direct investment. Some countries offer only short periods of patent protection for high technology products and/or lax enforcement of other intellectual property rights in order to encourage the transfer of technology to their domestic firms.

Tariff Negotiating Authority. Section 308 provides the only explicit tariff-negotiating authority offered by title III of the TTA. The president is authorized by this section to reach bilateral or multilateral agreements that reduce or eliminate the rate of duty on semiconductors, transistors, diodes, rectifiers, integrated circuits, and parts of computers. This provision ratifies a 1982 tariff agreement between the United States and Japan that eliminates tariffs on semiconductors and extends the benefits of this agreement to all other nations that receive most-favored-nation treatment. It also authorizes negotiations on a few additional items such as parts of computers that were not part of the bilateral accord, thus opening up the possibility of further tariff negotiations in high technology trade. This authority was used in November 1985 when the United States, Japan, and Canada announced a tri-partite agreement to eliminate tariffs on computer parts from all countries receiving MFN treatment. The authority will last until October 30, 1989, and could lead to further agreements.

Negotiating Objectives. The tariff authority is supplemented by detailed negotiating objectives. In terms of traditional concern for market access and tariff reduction, the TTA states that U.S. objectives are "to obtain and preserve the maximum openness with respect to international trade and investment in high technology products and related services" and "to obtain the reduction or elimination of all tariffs on, and other barriers to" U.S. exports of high technology products and related services.

The TTA goes on to make foreign industrial policies in the high technology field an object of concern for U.S. negotiators. The act declares that the United States will endeavor to obtain the elimination or reduction of, or compensation for "foreign industrial policies which distort international trade or investment" and "measures which deny national treatment or otherwise discriminate in favor of domestic high technology industries."

The U.S. concerns over industrial targeting are further reflected in the objectives of obtaining commitments that foreign countries "will not discourage government or private procurement of foreign high technology products and related services," and obtaining commitments to "foster the pursuit of joint scientific cooperation between companies, institutions or government entities" of the United States and its trading partners. Negotiators are directed to "ensure that access by all participants to the results of any such cooperative efforts should not be impaired."

Intellectual Property Rights

Intellectual property is a catchall term that encompasses any inventions, designs, and artistic creations that have been registered with government authorities for sale or use by their owner. These rights are protected by patents, trademarks, and copyrights. Among the many products that depend on sanctity of intellectual property rights are name-brand consumer goods, computer software, high technology products, motion pictures, musical recordings, books, pharmaceuticals, and chemicals.

Unlike the other new issues, intellectual property rights do not suffer for want of national and international rules. Section 337 of the Tariff Act of 1930 is the principal U.S. trade-remedy law that addresses this issue; under this statute the U.S. International Trade Commission can issue cease and desist or exclusion orders against foreign producers that violate patents or engage in other unfair trade acts. Other U.S. laws provide civil and criminal penalties for violations. Most foreign legal systems promise similar protection of these rights, and many countries have entered into bilateral, regional, and global agreements to which the United States is also a party. The Paris Convention for the Protection of Industrial Property dates back to 1883, and is administered by the World Intellectual Property Organization (WIPO). The United States is not a signatory to the Berne Convention for the Protection of Literary and Artistic Works of 1886, which is also administered by WIPO. Other international agreements on the subject include the Patent Cooperation Treaty, the International Patent Classification Agreement, and special conventions relating to microorganisms, phonograms, and satellite signals.

The many domestic and international guarantees of intellectual property rights have not prevented the global spread of counterfeiting, piracy, patent infringement, and other unfair trade acts. A study conducted by the U.S. International Trade Commission estimated that in 1982, counterfeiting and similar practices caused $49.2 million in lost export sales for U.S. firms, between $6 and $8 million in lost domestic sales, and 131,000 lost jobs.[7] Counterfeit goods are often shoddy and unsafe imitations that endanger consumers and threaten the reputation of the trademark or copyright owner.

Foreign violations of intellectual property rights became a priority issue of the House Energy and Commerce Committee during the 98th Congress. An extended series of investigative hearings on the matter revealed that counterfeiting affects virtually all consumer goods, as well as artistic and literary creations, agricultural chemicals, medical devices, and even parts used in the space shuttle. A report by the Subcommittee on Oversight and Investigations concluded that "in some countries, counterfeiting appears to have become the de facto national industrial development strategy."[8]

The uproar over intellectual property rights prodded the 98th Congress to pass the Trademark Counterfeiting Act of 1984, which imposes heavy criminal penalties for trafficking in counterfeit goods, and the Semiconductor Chip Protection Act of 1984, which grants a ten-year period of patent protection for semiconductor chips. Several sections of the TTA are intended to complement these efforts by establishing U.S. negotiating objectives in intellectual property rules and by providing penalties for countries that do not adequately enforce these rights.

Negotiating Objectives. Title III does not include a separate section on negotiating objectives for intellectual property rights, but incorporates these concerns among the other goals just discussed. One of the U.S. objectives in high technology is to obtain the elimination or reduction of foreign measures that "fail to provide adequate and effective means for foreign nationals to secure, exercise, and enforce exclusive rights in intellectual property." Negotiations are also to ensure that effective minimum safeguards are established "for the acquisition and enforcement of intellectual property rights and the property rights of proprietary data."

The renewed Generalized System of Preferences also addresses the intellectual property issue. U.S. negotiators will be able to use the tariff preferences of the GSP as leverage in their discussions with developing nations that do not offer full protection for U.S. intellectual property rights (see chapter 4).

Reciprocity and Retaliation

Establishing U.S. objectives in future negotiations is only the first step toward obtaining these goals; choosing the appropriate negotiating strategy and forum are more delicate problems. The TTA does not dictate any single tactical approach for the executive branch to use, nor does it provide explicit authority for the United States to enter into a new round of multilateral trade negotiations in the GATT. The TTA allows the executive branch to choose from three less sweeping alternatives. As is described in chapter 3, the United States may enter into bilateral agreements, such as the U.S.–Israeli free trade agreement. U.S. negotiators may also use the tariff preferences of the GSP as leverage in their discussions with developing nations (see chapter 4). A third option is to enforce U.S. rights through bi- and multilateral consultations, negotiations, and dispute-settlement procedures which, if not fruitful, can lead to unilateral retaliation. This alternative will be discussed in detail shortly.

Beginning in the 97th Congress (1981–1982), some members began to argue for making reciprocity the chief goal of U.S. trade policy. Most proposals centered on amending section 301 of the Trade Act of 1974 (the presidential retaliation authority) to make it a more aggressive policy instrument. The advocates of this approach viewed themselves as moderates, in that they neither called for unilateral market protection such as quotas or domestic content laws, nor did they believe that the existing adherence to multilateralism and liberal trade was sufficient for U.S. policy. By the standards of free trade purists, however, the form of reciprocity they called for would turn postwar U.S. trade policy on its head by rejecting the principles of comparative advantage and unconditional most-favored-nation treatment.

Before describing the operation of section 301 and the specific reciprocity proposals made in the 97th and 98th Congresses, it is first necessary to understand what reciprocity has meant in the history of U.S. trade policy. While reciprocity may rightly be called the touchstone of U.S. trade policy since the founding of the republic, the meaning of this term has undergone radical changes through the years.

The Meaning of Reciprocity in U.S. Trade History

The very first treaty signed by the United States incorporated the principle of bilateral and conditional reciprocity. In the 1778 treaty with the Kingdom of France, both parties pledged that any trade advantages that either nation had granted or might grant to a third party would be extended to the other "freely, if the concession was freely made, or on allowing the same compensation, if the concession was conditional." Similar language was included in nearly all U.S. commercial treaties negotiated in the ensuing century and a half. This formulation of reciprocity is known as *conditional most-favored-nation* treatment, so named because the treatment offered to the most favored nation would only be offered to other trading partners on the condition that they make an equivalent concession. It is distinguished from unconditional MFN treatment, which most European states followed after the midnineteenth century, under which concessions are automatically extended to all trading partners that receive MFN treatment.

In the conditional MFN approach, reciprocity meant bilateral bargaining. The system allowed each trading nation to keep a tight rein on the access it offered to other nations, but did little to advance commerce. The cumbersome process of negotiating for several different product areas in each bilateral agreement, together with the prevailing belief that U.S. industries needed protection from foreign competition, resulted in the conclusion of few agreements to liberalize trade. Until 1890, the United States negotiated only seven reciprocity agreements with its trading partners. Of these, only the treaties with Canada (1854) and Hawaii (1875) were ratified by the Senate.[9]

The conditional MFN approach was given a new twist in the 1890s, when the Congress approved commercial retaliation and negotiating authorities for the executive branch. The Tariff Act of 1890 (the McKinley Tariff) provided that the president could penalize countries that imposed "reciprocally unequal and unreasonable" duties on U.S. products by applying penalty duties on certain products from those countries. This authority was repealed in 1894, and replaced in the Tariff Act of 1897 (the Dingley Tariff) by an executive authority to negotiate tariff reduction agreements or impose penalty duties. The intent of these acts was to correct a perceived inequity in foreign tariff treatment of U.S. goods. Certain countries imposed high duties on U.S. exports, while the United States offered duty-free access for many of their products. In this sense, reciprocity meant offering tariff treatment that was substantially equivalent to that of the United States, or else facing the consequences.

This notion of reciprocity provided the executive branch with an aggressive means to pursue access to foreign markets, but it was a cumbersome tool for trade liberalization. U.S. negotiators still had to follow the often arduous process of bargaining product-by-product, and country-by-country. Only a handful of treaties were negotiated under these two acts. The agreements reached under the 1890 authority were unilaterally terminated by the United States in 1894, and the treaties negotiated under the 1897 authority were never ratified by the Senate.[10]

The limitations of the conditional MFN approach and the restricted negotiating authorities of 1890 and 1897 were all too apparent in the early twentieth century, when the United States emerged from its economic and political isolation to become a world class power. In a classic study of the problems with the conditional MFN approach, the newly created U.S. Tariff Commission (predecessor to the USITC) argued in 1919 that the policy "was natural so long as the United States kept aloof from foreign complications and was intent upon avoiding them,"[11] but that the new U.S. status demanded a more active and comprehensive approach. The Tariff Commission recommended that the United States abandon the conditional MFN approach and apply instead the principle of "equality of treatment" for all U.S. trading partners.

The Commission's recommendation was adopted in 1923, when Secretary of State Charles Evans Hughes declared that henceforth the United States would include an unconditional MFN clause in all bilateral commercial treaties. This pledge was made good in several treaties of friendship, commerce and navigation that were negotiated in that era, many of which are still in force. The policy was later embodied in the Reciprocal Trade Agreements Act of 1934, which provided the executive branch with the authority to negotiate tariff-reduction agreements that did not require congressional ratification.

Unconditional MFN treatment has since become the central principle of the GATT trading system. Under article 1 of the GATT, the "contracting parties" pledge that

> any advantage, favour, privilege or immunity granted by any contracting party to any product originating in or destined for any other country shall be accorded immediately and unconditionally to the like product originating in or destined for the territories of all other contracting parties.

With unconditional MFN treatment, reciprocity is an almost tautological concept, in which reciprocity is subjectively defined by the existence of the

GATT itself. To be a member of the GATT and to abide by its rules is to treat one's trading partners reciprocally. Reciprocity in the GATT cannot be viewed in bilateral terms. It is based on the series of trade agreements freely negotiated among GATT members. Reciprocity is not tied to any single identifiable bargain, nor to equivalent duty treatment on a product-for-product basis.

The only significant exceptions to the rule of unconditional MFN treatment in the GATT are free trade arrangements or customs unions that must meet certain criteria (see chapter 3), the special dispensation provided by the "enabling clause" for the beneficiary developing countries of the Generalized System of Preferences (see chapter 4), and "code reciprocity" in special agreements such as the GATT Subsidies Code (see chapter 6).

The "New" Reciprocity

The reciprocity proposals advanced in the 97th and 98th Congresses bore a much stronger resemblance to reciprocity as it was practiced in 1890 than they did to the modern GATT meaning of the term. Frustrated by the ever-growing U.S. trade deficit with Japan and other competitors, and convinced that it was largely the product of unequal levels of protection applied by the United States and its principal trading partners, Senator John C. Danforth (Rep.-Mo.) and his confederates introduced a host of reciprocity bills. These were intended to pressure U.S. trading partners into providing equivalent competitive opportunities for U.S. exporters. Foreign countries would be given a choice between reducing their trade barriers to the levels imposed by the United States or facing the prospect that U.S. barriers would be raised in retaliation. Some proposals also contemplated applying this meaning of reciprocity to trade in services and trade-related investment.

In terms of GATT principles, the heresy of the new reciprocity is the contention that reciprocity should be equated with market access as measured by comparing barriers at a sectoral or product level. In its more advanced form, the new reciprocity even demands that the actual trade balances be equivalent. The break that the new reciprocity made with the status quo meaning of the term was recognized by Senator Robert Dole (then chairman of the Senate Finance Committee) in an article published in the *New York Times*. The senator opined that:

> reciprocity means a dramatic change from the "most-favored-nation" principle. It means that other countries should provide us with trade and investment opportunities equal not simply to what they afford their other "most-favored" trading partners but equal to what we offer them and reciprocity should be assessed not by what agreements promise but by actual results—by changes in the balance of trade and growth in investment between ourselves and our major economic partners.[12]

From the liberal trader's point of view, pursuing "sectoral reciprocity" in merchandise trade is politically hazardous and economically unsound. If the United States were to retaliate unilaterally against another GATT member's barriers by reneging on its own binding market liberalization, the U.S. trading partner would be within its rights to either seek compensation from the United States or to counterretaliate. If two trading partners begin a cycle of retaliation and counterretaliation, there is a real danger of unraveling the entire fabric of reciprocal tariff agreements. In the words of one critic, this is "a prescription for anarchy."[13]

In economic terms, pursuing sectoral reciprocity in merchandise trade means discarding the notion of comparative advantage and overturning the GATT approach to trade liberalization. The reciprocity advocates can indeed point to the fact that the European Community has historically imposed much tighter restrictions on steel than has the United States, or that Japan is more restrictive in citrus and beef products. They might also note similar disparities in the U.S. trade regime, such as high barriers for imported textiles, shoes, fruits, and vegetables. Emphasizing these apparent inequities, however, misses the point of the GATT approach to trade liberalization. The goal is to achieve an overall reciprocity in market access rather than identical trade regimes at the product or sectoral level. The GATT system has been largely successful in attaining this objective.

The apparent inequities in sectoral market access offered by different trading partners are an artifact of the GATT negotiating methods. Although the trade concessions negotiated in the GATT are implemented multilaterally, most are originally hammered out in a bilateral fashion. For example, the United States might offer a tariff concession to Japan for radios in exchange for a Japanese tariff reduction in cigarettes. If this bargain is struck, the binding tariff reductions enacted by both countries are unconditionally available to all other countries that receive MFN treatment. Trade negotiators make these deals on the basis of the comparative advantage their countries have in the products under consideration, and are usually not concerned with achieving tariff parity in sectors or identical product areas. U.S. trade negotiators in the Tokyo Round were instructed to seek "substantially equivalent competitive opportunities" in some individual sectors of interest, but this goal was moderated by a stipulation that such objectives should only be obtained "to the extent consistent with the objective of maximizing overall economic benefits to the United States." Specific sectoral negotiations such as the 1982 U.S.–Japanese agreement eliminating duties on most semiconductors are the exception rather than the rule. It should come as no surprise, then, that this system often results in asymmetrical tariff structures.

While the foregoing argument against sectoral reciprocity may be neatly applied to merchandise trade, some argue that the reciprocity approach could be more useful in investment rules and the services trade. Because these new issues are not subject to international agreements at present, applying the rule of reciprocity would be less likely to disrupt the trading system. A sectoral reciprocity approach in the new issues might offer U.S. negotiators a benchmark against which they could gauge their progress in bilateral or multilateral talks. From the perspective of some U.S. trading partners, however, pursuing reciprocity in services and investments would mean opening their economies before local infant industries could grow competitive.

Reciprocity and the Reagan Administration

The three dozen or so reciprocity bills introduced in the 97th and 98th Congresses varied widely according to focus and administrative procedures, but they all shared a common intent: to force the executive branch into a more aggressive posture in dealing with foreign trade barriers. The tight rein placed on executive discretion in many of these proposals stemmed from a perennial congressional concern that the executive branch allows foreign policy concerns to inhibit it from enforcing U.S. rights. Several of the reciprocity bills would have required the executive branch to undertake studies of foreign barriers, and to justify any failure on its part to negotiate vigorously for the removal or reduction of these barriers. Other proposals would almost automatically force the president to retaliate against any foreign barrier that he determined burdened or restricted U.S. trade, or to submit "mirror legislation" to the U.S. Congress that would establish an identical restriction in the U.S. market for the country in question.

The Reagan administration opposed proposals that would reduce the discretion of the executive branch in pursuing U.S. trade interests abroad and require sector-specific reciprocity, but it was careful not to dismiss the reciprocity initiative out of hand. The application of this approach in services and investment issues was attractive for U.S. negotiators, who hoped that it would provide them with the leverage they needed to press for new international rules in these areas. The administration was also mindful that embracing the new reciprocity would help fend off the enactment of unilateral and protectionist alternatives such as quota bills or domestic-content requirements. For these reasons, the administration worked with Senator Danforth to craft a compromise proposal that would strengthen the negotiating and retaliatory authority of the executive branch without requiring any precise course of action.

Once the administration was satisfied that its concerns were reflected in the bill, it supported the Danforth initiative. This legislation evolved into the International Trade and Investment Act (title III of the TTA). Besides establishing negotiating objectives, the bill also amends section 301 of the Trade Act of 1974 to provide the U.S. negotiators with explicit authority to ferret out foreign barriers to U.S. exports and investments, negotiate for their removal or reduction, and retaliate if the barriers are not removed or reduced. The legislation tightens the procedures used in section 301 cases and establishes an extensive annual reporting requirement on all foreign barriers to U.S. exports.

Section 301

Section 301 of the Trade Act of 1974—the presidential retaliation authority—gives the president the authority to take all "appropriate action" to obtain the removal of foreign trade barriers. While section 301 is technically a trade-remedy law, it differs from the escape clause and the antisubsidy and antidumping statutes in several respects.

First and foremost, section 301 does not deal exclusively with imports. While section 301 can be applied in cases involving unfairly traded imports into the U.S. market—cases that are normally in the jurisdiction of other trade laws—it is primarily intended to deal with the problems faced by U.S. exporters. The law may be used to negotiate for reduction or removal of foreign barriers to U.S. goods, or to fight foreign subsidies for exports into third-country markets.

The statute may be employed to enforce any U.S. trade rights that are violated by another country's practices, whether or not these rights are formally and explicitly established in the GATT or other trade agreements. Specifically, the statute provides that section 301 may be used to take action against any act, policy, or practice of a foreign country that the president determines:

1. is inconsistent with the provisions of, or otherwise denies benefits to the United States under, any trade agreement, or
2. is unjustifiable, unreasonable, or discriminatory and burdens or restricts United States commerce.

In contrast to the fairly strict statutory definitions provided in U.S. trade law for dumping and subsidization (see chapter 6), these definitions leave a tremendous degree of latitude. The United States may use section 301 in some instances where there is no established international agreement, where the relevance of an existing agreement may not be clear, or even conceivably in cases where an agreement exists, but the United States is not a signatory. Under the "unreasonable, unjustifiable, or discriminatory" standard, explicit international agreements are a sufficient but not a necessary condition for initiating an investigation.

The statute revolves around governmental negotiations rather than the quasi-judicial domestic proceedings that are characteristic of the trade-remedy laws. The emphasis on consultation and negotiation stems from the statute's concern with foreign governmental practices. These matters cannot reasonably be addressed without directly consulting the foreign government in question.

U.S. firms may formally petition the USTR to initiate section 301 proceedings in order to pursue a complaint with foreign governments. The petition must explain the nature of the foreign practice that allegedly violates U.S. rights, and whether the policy involves unfair import restrictions or export practices. The USTR then has forty-five days to determine whether to initiate an investigation. To avoid redundancy, the USTR will not accept petitions concerning matters that are already under investigation in another trade-remedy proceeding, such as the antisubsidy statute. If the petition is accepted, the USTR simultaneously investigates the matter, and consults with the foreign government on the issues raised in the petition.[14] At this point, the complaint has become a matter of government interest, and the petitioner no longer has essential control over the process.

The USTR has complete discretion to accept or reject petitions. Acceptance of a petition by the USTR is a somewhat weightier matter than the equivalent action taken by the Department of Commerce in antidumping or countervailing duty cases. When Commerce accepts a petition, it is merely making an objective decision that the petition is in good form (that is, it contains the type of information necessary to initiate an investigation), without passing judgment on the validity of the charges. By contrast, the USTR exercises greater legal and political judgment when it accepts a petition under section 301. The USTR often makes an initial attempt to verify the allegations laid out in a petition before accepting it, and acceptance means that the USTR has concluded in at least a preliminary fashion that the issue raised in the petition appears legally valid. The USTR might also reject a petition if, in its judgment, the case might lead to unwanted political complications for the United States.

The USTR's role in section 301 cases is qualitatively different from that of the Department of Commerce or the U.S. International Trade Commission in the other trade-remedy laws. Whereas Commerce and the USITC are intended to deal with cases solely on their objective merits as defined by the relevant statutes, the USTR's task is more subjective. It must not only investigate the petitioner's allegations, and determine whether a legal right of the United States has been violated, but also be prepared to devise and pursue a negotiated solution with a foreign government. The USTR both adjudicates and advocates in these cases.

Although the Trade Act of 1974 gives the USTR nearly complete formal control over section 301 cases, the USTR consults with other agencies through the interagency Section 301 Committee. This committee is composed of representatives from each of the federal agencies that are directly or indirectly concerned with trade policy, and is part of the network of interagency consultative groups that advise the president on such matters as cases arising under the escape clause (see chapter 5). As in the case of escape clause proceedings, the agencies represented on this committee offer a range of institutional perspectives, some of which might tend to militate against taking a hard-line position with U.S. trading partners.

There is no provision in the statute for judicial review of the executive's decisions by the Court of International Trade, nor does it provide for a congressional override. The law is designed to maximize the authority of the president and the USTR, and minimize the power of technical or judicial bodies.

Section 301 and Dispute Settlement in the GATT

One of the principal functions of the GATT is to provide a forum in which the member states can settle any disputes that might arise concerning their trading rights. Dispute-settlement proceedings in the GATT fall under the jurisdiction of Article XXIII, which does not actually define any specific procedures for the institution to follow. These questions were left to evolve among the members through trial and error. During the early years of the GATT, a system emerged that revolved around panels of experts. These panels, although composed of governmental representatives, were intended to act in an independent and impartial manner. The GATT panels established a reputation for objectivity, and through their deliberations they contributed to the development of GATT law.

The panel system operated fairly smoothly until the 1960s, when growing rifts among the GATT signatories threatened the consensus on basic trade principles. With the emergence of the developing countries and the Western European states as major blocs with contending interests, it became increasingly difficult to resolve divisive issues. The increasing politicization of trade brought the objectivity of the GATT panels into question, and the proceedings themselves fell into disuse.

Additional rules for the GATT system were created with the proliferation of special GATT codes in the Tokyo Round negotiations. These agreements deal with specific issues such as export subsidies, government procurement policies, and customs valuation methods. While the codes have helped to define the rights and obligations of their signatories, they have also served to complicate the dispute settlement problem. Of the eleven codes negotiated during the Tokyo Round, no two lay out identical dispute-settlement provisions. Furthermore, the codes have only been accepted by some countries, and their relevance for nonsignatories is in question.

The institutional structure of the GATT is not well equipped to reach or enforce definitive solutions to problems. The GATT is not the embodiment of the rule of law at an international level. It is erroneous, in fact, to speak of the "member states" of the GATT, for the organization consists instead of contracting parties who agree to play by its rules, rather than members who must abide by its rulings. The signatories to the GATT interpret the rights and obligations conferred by the General Agreement in a given set of circumstances, and can authorize a nation to take countermeasures against another nation's policies that are found to violate the rules. In actual practice, this virtually never happens. The GATT operates on the principle of consensus, which effectively offers a unit veto to each and every country. Even if a nation loses its case before a GATT panel, the panel's report is not official until it has been unanimously adopted. The GATT's dispute-settlement role is also weakened by the difficulties encountered in assembling qualified panels composed of unbiased experts.

Section 301 is in large part a congressional response to the shortcomings of the GATT dispute-settlement mechanism. It is intended to complement the formal GATT procedures rather than to replace them. The statute might best be seen as a procedural overlay to the U.S. negotiating powers, through which domestic industries may formally petition their government for action in the GATT or elsewhere. Appearing first as section 252 of the Trade Expansion Act of 1962 and later recast as section 301 of the Trade Act of 1974, the "presidential retaliation" authority was designed to spell out the president's power to enforce U.S. trade rights through negotiations and retaliation. The legislative history of the law, including the amendments made in 1979 and 1984, indicate a growing congressional interest in encouraging presidential use of this authority. The chief intent of the 1979 amendments was to put specific time limits on the USTR's recommendations to the president for action under the law, while the 1984 amendments—as will be discussed shortly—clarify the applicability of the law and encourage the USTR to use it more aggressively.

Section 301 is not intended to serve exclusively as a domestic complement to the GATT; it may also be used in cases outside of the GATT. This may happen when the country in question is not a GATT signatory, or when the issue at hand is not covered by the GATT or its codes. In such instances, the United States will pursue its case on the basis of whatever other agreement may be appropriate. For example, many of the bilateral treaties of friendship, commerce, and navigation to which the United States subscribes provide dispute-settlement procedures.

The statute sets deadlines for the USTR to either resolve the problem or make a recommendation to the president for further action. The length of time available to the USTR depends on the nature of the dispute. If the complaint concerns export subsidies, the USTR has seven months before it must make a recommendation to the president. When the issue involves other matters covered by the GATT Subsidies Code, the USTR has eight months. Disputes involving other trade agreements reached during the Tokyo Round must be resolved within thirty days of the conclusion of dispute-settlement procedures. These timetables track the periods established in the respective GATT codes. In any matter that does not fit any of these three categories—particularly issues that are not yet the subject of formal international agreements—the USTR has twelve months.

If the issues are covered by a trade agreement and are not resolved during any consultation period which may be specified in the agreement, USTR must promptly request that formal dispute settlement proceedings be initiated. The exact nature of these proceedings depends on the provisions of the trade agreement that is alleged to be violated. The GATT and its various codes provide formal procedures for resolving disputes among their signatories. A GATT panel is established to hear the arguments of both sides and to issue a report on its findings. A panel report must be adopted by the GATT contracting parties before it is official, a stipulation that encourages the losing party to block adoption through dilatory maneuvers. Although the GATT may decide in favor of the United States position, it does not have any independent authority to impose sanctions or enforce its decisions. The practical consequence of a GATT ruling favorable to the United States is that if the other party does not abide by the decision, the United States is then free to take unilateral action.

While these multilateral proceedings are taking place, the United States and the foreign government may continue to attempt a negotiated resolution. The U.S. negotiators could conceivably offer concessions to the other party as a means of reaching a broader solution to the dispute, but this is not generally done. Any tariff concessions they might offer to the other party would require full congressional approval, although nontariff concessions could be submitted for expedited congressional approval on the fast track.[15] For the most part, the burden of concessions is placed on the other country.

Retaliation under Section 301

If there is no solution before the relevant deadlines expire, the USTR must recommend what action, under section 301, the president should take on matters raised in the investigation. The president then has twenty-one days to decide what action, if any, to take. Section 301 gives the executive branch a broad scope for retaliatory action. The president is authorized to

1. suspend, withdraw, or prevent the application of, or refrain from proclaiming, benefits of trade agreement concessions to carry out a trade agreement with the foreign country or instrumentality involved; and

2. impose duties or other import restrictions on the products of, and fees or restrictions on the services of, such foreign country or instrumentality for such time as he determines appropriate.

The retaliation can be applied to all countries on a nondiscriminatory basis, or to a single country or group of countries on a discriminatory basis. Moreover, the retaliation may be directed against goods or services other than those identified in the petition. In this way, the United States can target the retaliatory authority at the sectors that are most likely to get results.

The retaliatory powers have been rarely used, however. Until 1985, the president almost invariably determined that the appropriate response would be to continue any proceedings that may already have been initiated and are considered appropriate to pursue further.

In the ten years between enactment of the Trade Act of 1974 and the end of 1984, forty-seven investigations were initiated under section 301. During that period, not a single one led to direct retaliation under the statute. The first use of the authority came when President Reagan ordered that increased duties be assessed against European pasta in June 1985, in retaliation for the European Community's (EC) practice of offering tariff preferences on citrus products to certain Mediterranean countries. A case involving Argentine violations of a bilateral agreement led the United States to rescind a previous tariff concession on corned beef. For technical reasons, however, the concession was withdrawn under a separate authority. The only other examples of retaliation are indirect. Six cases were initiated in 1981 involving stainless steel from Austria, Belgium, France, Italy, Sweden, and the United Kingdom. After formal consultations in the GATT failed to resolve the matter, the president requested in 1982 that the USITC initiate escape-clause proceedings. The USITC found that imports of stainless steel caused serious injury to the U.S. industry, and in 1983 President Reagan ordered higher duties on some speciality steel products and import quotas on others for a four-year period. In another instance of indirect retaliation, President Carter requested that the Congress respond to a border broadcasting dispute with Canada by enacting mirror legislation. This was eventually done in the TTA, as is described shortly.

The fact that section 301 has not been used as a retaliatory instrument does not mean that it fails to serve its intended purpose. The real value of the statute lies in its potential for resolving disputes without resorting to retaliation. Most petitioners wish to see a change in the other country's behavior, rather than new restrictions in U.S. trade policy. An ideal case will lead to a mutually agreeable solution long before it reaches the president's desk. The great majority of cases, however, are subject to prolonged consultations and dispute-settlement proceedings that are sometimes subject to dilatory maneuvers. Some cases have lasted more than a decade without being resolved.

The subject matter of the cases investigated thus far is interesting. The most frequently cited complaint of petitioners involves EC agricultural policies, including tariff and nontariff barriers and export subsidies on agricultural products that are sold either to the United States or third-country markets. These investigations have focused on wheat flour, egg albumin, sugar, malt, poultry, pasta, citrus products, canned fruit, and raisins, and altogether account for one fourth of the section 301 investigations initiated thus far. Several investigations have involved matters that are not the subject of explicit agreements or established international rules. This is most notable in cases involving services, including insurance in Argentina, the Soviet Union, and South Korea; courier services in Argentina; shipping in Guatemala; and even the pricing policies of European satellite launchers.

Section 301 and the New Issues

The TTA amends section 301 in order to make the statute a more useful tool for pressuring U.S. trading partners. The amendments highlight the new issues of services and trade-related investment, and alter the law's definitions to specifically cover these matters. The TTA also makes procedural changes in the law that are intended to strengthen the authority of the Office of the U.S. Trade Representative.

New Definitions

The act provides new definitions for section 301 that serve two purposes. First, they attempt to clarify the operative language of the law, especially three key terms that were originally left undefined in the Trade Act of 1974: *unreasonable*, *unjustifiable*, and *discriminatory*. Second, the definitions strengthen the new U.S. negotiating objectives by equating trade not only with the exchange of goods and services, but also with investment in enterprises that lead to trade in goods or services. This extends the scope of the USTR's authority.

The legislative history of the term *unreasonable* indicates that the Congress intended that the word transcend the strict letter of international law. According to a 1979 report of the Senate Finance Committee, *unreasonable* referred to restrictions that "are not necessarily inconsistent with trade agreements."[16] Section 304 of the Trade and Tariff Act codifies and extends this definition by equating *unreasonable* with:

> any act, policy, or practice which, while not necessarily in violation of or inconsistent with the international legal rights of the United States, is otherwise deemed to be unfair and inequitable. The term includes, but is not limited to, any act, policy, or practice which denies fair and equitable—
> (A) market opportunities;
> (B) opportunities for the establishment of an enterprise; or
> (C) provision of adequate and effective protection of intellectual property rights.

The definition offered for *unjustifiable* is even more explicit on the subject of investment issues. The term "means any act, policy, or practice which is in violation of, or inconsistent with, the international legal rights of the United States." The law states that it "includes, but is not limited to, any act, policy, or practice . . . which denies national or most-favored-nation treatment, the right of establishment, or protection of intellectual property rights." National treatment is equal to the treatment available to the citizens of a country. It is distinct from most-favored-nation treatment, under which a country receives the best treatment accorded to any other foreign country.

The U.S. demands for national treatment in services and trade-related investment are reiterated in the definition of *discriminatory*, which includes "any act, policy, or practice which denies national or most-favored-nation treatment to United States goods, services, or investment."

These definitions take on new importance with the USTR's emphasis on the service sector and trade-related investment. Unless and until more comprehensive international standards are established in these areas, the United States will be able to determine and apply its own interpretations of *unreasonable* and *discriminatory*. This may prod other countries into negotiating international service and investment codes, particularly if the United States attempts to push aggressively for its self-defined rights.

If any doubts remain that these new issues fall within the scope of section 301, such doubts are erased by the definition for commerce. According to the act,

> the term *commerce* includes, but is not limited to—
> (A) services (including transfers of information) associated with international trade, whether or not such services are related to specific goods, and
> (B) foreign direct investment by United States persons with implications for trade in goods or services.

The services aspect of this definition is not, in fact, a significant change over the previous legislation. The Trade Agreements Act of 1979 defined commerce in section 301 to include "services associated with international trade, whether or not such services are related to specific products." The only change brought about by the new language is the phrase indicating that "transfers of information" are included under this definition.

By contrast, the inclusion of foreign direct investment in the meaning of *commerce* is new. To date, no cases pursued under section 301 have revolved solely around investment issues. The new definition significantly expands the meaning of commerce and, by implication, the responsibilities of the USTR. The scope of the USTR's retaliatory power, however, might be limited to those investments that actually lead to transnational trade in goods and services.

Retaliatory Authority in Services

Section 304 of the TTA amends section 301 to allow direct retaliation against countries that deny U.S. firms the right to invest in their service sectors. It states that the president may restrict or deny the issuance of "service sector authorizations" (that is, licenses to provide services) issued under federal law. With this new retaliatory authority, the president may keep foreign firms from marketing their services in the United States. The retaliatory authority is complicated, however, by the fact that state governments have sole regulatory powers over the insurance industry and have exclusive or shared authority in regulating most other services. For this reason, any retaliation against foreign providers of services may require close coordination between the federal and state governments. The TTA further stipulates that this authority will not apply to licenses that were already issued prior to the initiation of an investigation, a loophole that could dilute much of the law's impact.

Retaliation for Export Performance Requirements

Section 307 of the TTA gives the USTR the authority "to respond to any export performance requirements of any foreign country or instrumentality that adversely affect the economic interest of the United States." The USTR is directed to enter into consultations with the countries in question, and "may impose duties or other import restrictions" if it does not obtain satisfactory results. The restrictions can include "the exclusion from entry into the United States of products subject to such requirements." This retaliatory authority provides the USTR with a potentially awesome weapon. The only limitation on the USTR's use of this authority is self-restraint.

The authority is subject to a grandfather clause, under which the sanctions may not be applied to exports produced in any direct investment abroad made by U.S. firms or individuals before the provision's date of enactment. The proviso was added to accommodate U.S. automobile manufacturers that have large investments overseas. It appears to be inconsistent with the principle of national treatment—one of the U.S. objectives set out in the TTA—in that it allows more favorable treatment for overseas subsidiaries of U.S. firms than is accorded to foreign enterprises with no American ownership.

Procedural Changes in Section 301

The TTA alters the procedures followed in section 301 cases. The amendments increase the independence and negotiating authority of the USTR.

Initiation of Investigations. The original section 301 authority allowed the USTR to initiate investigations upon petition from domestic parties. Some trade lawyers interpreted the statute to mean that the USTR also had the authority to "self-initiate" (that is, to initiate cases on its own motion), but the point was moot because the USTR never attempted to do so. Section 304 of the TTA amends section 301 to state that the USTR may initiate investigations "in order to advise the President concerning the exercise of the President's authority under section 301." As is discussed shortly, this self-initiation authority was used for the first time in September 1985. If the executive branch uses this new tool regularly to achieve its international trade objectives, then this provision may ultimately prove to be among the most significant sections of the TTA.

Delays in the Initiation of International Consultations. Under the earlier section 301 authority, the USTR technically began international consultations on the same date that any investigation was initiated. The TTA provides that the USTR may delay consultations for up to ninety days following the initiation of an investigation. This delay will allow time to verify and improve the petition, and to ensure that the USTR has an adequate basis for consultations. If the USTR does delay the initiation of consultations, then the deadlines for the USTR's recommendation to the president are rolled forward.

Other Provisions of the Act

Sectoral Reciprocity

Several of the reciprocity bills introduced in the 97th and 98th Congresses were specifically directed at individual sectors or products for which foreign barriers were alleged to be disproportionately high when compared to U.S. barriers for the same goods. Most of the sectoral reciprocity bills were rejected, but two such initiatives were enacted in other sections of the TTA.

Wine Reciprocity. The U.S. wine grape industry has complained in recent years that it is caught in a squeeze between competition from France and Italy, and foreign import barriers that tower above the U.S. tariff wall. The Congress responded to the industry's complaints by modifying the rules regarding standing in trade-remedy cases (see chapter 6), and by passing the Wine Equity and Export Expansion Act of 1984 (title IX of the Trade and Tariff Act). As originally proposed in 1983, the wine equity bill would have put the U.S. Trade Representative in a negotiating straitjacket by directing that he negotiate foreign tariffs on U.S. wine down to the tariff levels imposed by the United States. If this goal was not achieved by January 1, 1986, the president would be required by law to use his authority under section 301 to raise U.S. duties on wine to the level imposed by the exporting country. The Reagan administration opposed this proposal strenuously, arguing that because the executive branch has no explicit congressional mandate to offer tariff reductions to other countries in exchange for their concessions on wine—and the legislation itself made no provision for such negotiating authority—retaliation against foreign wine barriers would simply lead to counterretaliation against some other U.S. export.[17]

The Congress responded to the administration's objections by allowing for greater executive discretion in the wine-reciprocity negotiations. Title IX of the TTA mandates the USTR to investigate the barriers imposed by all "major wine trading countries" on U.S. wine exports, consult with the Congress and the industry over the strategy it will employ to remove these barriers, and take the appropriate measures to remove them. The act does not require that any specific retaliation be taken against countries that do not reduce their barriers, nor does it provide the USTR with the authority to offer tariff concessions on other products.

After soliciting comments from grape growers and other interested parties, the USTR named six "major wine trading countries" in September 1985: Canada, Japan, Mexico, South Korea, Taiwan, and Trinidad and Tobago. These countries allegedly erect unreasonable barriers to wine imports in the form of prohibitively high tariffs, state monopolies, or import-licensing schemes. The USTR began to enter into bilateral consultations with each nation in late 1985 to seek the reduction or elimination of their barriers, and reached an early agreement with Taiwan. The president has the power under section 301 to retaliate against the remaining nations if they are unwilling to make concessions, but it is not clear yet whether any of the consultations will actually lead to formal dispute settlement proceedings or threats of retaliation under section 301.

Canadian Border Broadcasting and Mirror Legislation. The only other sector-specific reciprocity measure in the TTA is a provision that denies U.S. firms the right to deduct the expense of advertising on Canadian TV channels or radio stations from their income taxes. This provision stems from a section 301 case filed by U.S. broadcasters in 1978. Their petition complained that the Canadian tax code denied deductions for Canadian taxpayers who purchased advertising services from U.S. broadcasters when the advertising was directed primarily at the Canadian market. According to the U.S. broadcasters, this cost them approximately $25 million per year in lost revenues. In 1980, President Carter determined under section 301 that this practice was unreasonable and imposed a burden on U.S. commerce, and asked that the Congress pass mirror legislation in retaliation. This proposal was stalled for three years by new negotiating initiatives, but was later reintroduced by the Reagan administration.

Section 232 of the TTA amends the Internal Revenue Code to deny deductions "for any expenses of an advertisement carried by a foreign broadcasting undertaking and directed primarily to a market in the United States." The legislation specifies that this provision only applies to "foreign broadcasting undertakings in a country which denies a similar deduction ... with a United States broadcasting undertaking." The penalty imposed by this mirror legislation enters into effect with the 1985 tax year, and will no longer apply if the Canadian legislation is repealed. As of this writing, neither country has blinked.

Annual Report on Foreign Trade Barriers

Several of the reciprocity bills proposed during the 97th and 98th Congresses would have required that the executive branch prepare regular reports on the barriers erected by foreign countries to U.S. investment and exports of goods and services. Some proposals would have allowed or even required the president to take action against these barriers by proposing fast-track legislation, such as establishing mirror-image restrictions. Other bills would simply have required that the president explain what action was taken to remove these barriers, or justify any executive inaction. In either case, the intent of the reporting requirement would be to pressure the executive branch into pursuing U.S. market access and other goals more aggressively.

The Reagan administration objected to the proposed reporting requirement, arguing that such reports would be tantamount to the unilateral conviction of foreign governments without due process under the trade-remedy laws. The reports would establish a presumption of guilt for the practices that they identify even before a section 301 investigation has begun, and would render indirect assistance to potential domestic petitioners.

Despite these objections, section 303 of the Trade Act mandates the Trade Policy Committee (TPC), which is chaired by the USTR, to identify and analyze foreign barriers to U.S. trade and investment. The TPC is to collect its findings in an annual *National Trade Estimate* to be submitted to the Congress, the first of these estimates being due on or before October 30, 1985. These reports are to focus on all foreign acts, policies, or practices that constitute significant barriers to U.S. exports of goods or services, including agricultural commodities and intellectual property. The TPC is also to report on foreign barriers to U.S. direct investment, especially when this investment has implications for trade in goods or services. The report must make an estimate of the trade-distorting impact of these barriers, and should include information on any action taken (or the reasons for not taking action) to eliminate them. The intent of the authors of this amendment is to increase the political pressure on the White House. If the president identifies a trade barrier but does nothing to remove it, he will be liable for severe criticism.

The first *National Trade Estimate* was released on October 30, 1985. This catalog—dubbed the "section 303 report"—identified dozens of significant trade barriers erected by thirty-four industrialized and developing countries. The report offered several caveats. First, it cautioned that the inclusion of a barrier in the list did not signify that the practice was actually illegal. High tariff barriers, for example, are only illegal if they exceed the binding maximum limits that a country has agreed to in earlier multilateral trade negotiations. The report focused on the effect rather than the legality of barriers, defining foreign trade barriers as "policies designed to restrict or prevent the international exchange of goods and services."[18] By the same token, the report stated that failure to list any given practice engaged in by another country did not mean that the practice in question was not an unfair trade barrier. The report excluded nonmarket economies (that is, communist countries), because trade barriers erected by these countries are of a fundamentally different nature, and did not deal extensively with the smaller developing nations.

It would be a mistake to view the section 303 report as a catalog for future self-initiations under section 301 by the USTR. On the release of the document Ambassador Yeutter stated that it "shows why we need a multilateral round of negotiations."[19] The U.S. government would clearly prefer to see the barriers reduced through liberalizing negotiations, rather than by an essentially coercive process. Still, the report does present an impressive U.S. shopping list for future negotiations.

The section 303 reporting requirement is complemented by amendments to the International Investment Survey Act of 1976, a statute that directs the executive branch to make periodic reports on foreign investment in the United States and investments by U.S. citizens and corporations overseas. This law is renamed the "International Investment and Trade in Services Survey Act," with services included in its reporting requirements. The amendment also calls for benchmark surveys to be conducted every five years to gather information on trade in services between unaffiliated U.S. persons (natural or juridical) and foreign persons.

Consultations with State and Local Governments

The USTR has a network of advisory committees for consultations with the private sector, Congress, and other agencies of the federal government.[20] The TTA extends the scope of these networks by establishing committees for "the non-Federal governmental sector," meaning state and local governments. The president is authorized to establish policy advisory committees composed of representatives from state and local governments, as well as intergovernmental policy advisory committees.

The purpose of these committees is to provide a consulting forum with the federal government on matters of trade policy, including the regulatory authority of nonfederal government units. Like the existing committees, these new committees can also work in reverse, with the USTR using them to request advice, assistance, or information. The TTA directs the USTR to consult with these and other advisory committees when it prepares the annual *National Trade Estimate*.

The state advisory committees will have an important role in the development and execution of U.S. policy on trade in services. Because the state governments are largely responsible for licensing and regulating service firms such as banks and insurance companies, federal efforts to pursue reciprocity in services will require close coordination with the states. Unless the state regulatory agencies are willing to cooperate with the USTR by carrying through with threats of retaliation (for example, denying licenses to foreign insurance companies), the USTR will not have a credible means of pressuring foreign governments. Conversely, the USTR will have to coordinate with the states if any concessions in these sectors are to be offered to foreign countries.

Service Industries Development Program

One of the key points raised during the debate on trade in services is the absence of comprehensive and reliable data. Services are still dealt with as a residual category in balance of payments statistics. Without reliable information on the magnitude and diversity of service transactions, U.S. trade negotiators have inadequate guidance for any negotiations in this area.

Section 306 of the TTA directs the secretary of commerce to establish a Service Industries Development Program. The purposes of this program are to develop policies for increasing the competitiveness of U.S. service industries, develop a data base, collect and analyze information on the international operations and competitiveness of U.S. service industries, conduct a research program on service-related issues and problems, and carry out sectoral studies of domestic service industries.

Impact of the TTA's Provisions

In the year following enactment of the TTA, section 301 moved up to take a prominent place in the U.S. trade strategy. On September 7, 1985, the Reagan administration used the new authority conferred by the TTA to self-initiate investigations of Brazil's informatics policy, Korean insurance, and Japanese tobacco restrictions. At the same time, the White House set a December deadline for the resolution of two outstanding section 301 cases involving the European Community's barriers to U.S. canned fruits and raisins, and Japanese imports of U.S. leather goods. A month later, another case was self-initiated against South Korea, this time centering on the country's protection for U.S. intellectual property rights (patents, trademarks, and copyrights). Another first came in late 1985, when President Reagan used his authority under section 301 to levy additional duties on imported European pasta.[21] This action was taken in retaliation for the discriminatory tariff preferences that the European Community extends to certain Mediterranean countries, and represented the first time that section 301 had ever been used to retaliate directly against a U.S. trading partner.

Why did the United States begin to play hardball with the section 301 authority? The Reagan administration felt it needed to take decisive action in order to assert its authority both at home and abroad. The administration's hopes for a new round of multilateral trade negotiations in the GATT were frustrated by foreign resistance to the agenda proposed by the United States, and congressional demands for immediate action against unfair foreign trade practices. The announcement also coincided with President Reagan's refusal to provide import relief under the escape clause to the U.S. shoe industry (see chapter 5). By announcing the new actions under section 301, the White House hoped to convince U.S. trading partners that it was willing to pursue its negotiating objectives inside or outside of a new multilateral round, demonstrate its seriousness to Capitol Hill, and deflect criticism for its refusal to protect the footwear industry.

The question naturally arises, is the increased use of section 301 simply a quick fix, or does it set a pattern for future U.S. trade policy? The answer depends on whether further progress is made towards inaugurating the new round of negotiations. If the United States is unable to achieve its negotiating objectives through multilateral agreements, it will resort to other alternatives. Section 301 provides one approach; the next two chapters discuss other ways that the United States might bargain with its trading partners.

Notes

1. See testimony of Ambassador William Brock, cited in note 8, chapter 1.

2. Estimates by the International Monetary Fund, as cited in U.S. Government, *U.S. National Study on Trade in Services; A Submission by the United States Government to the General Agreement on Tariffs and Trade* (n.p.: U.S. Government, 1983), p. 8.

3. See data of the Futures Research Division, Security Pacific Bank, *The Wall Street Journal*, August 7, 1985, p. 19.

4. See Joanne Guth, "National Studies on Services Trade Issues Lay Groundwork for multilateral Discussion," *International Economic Review* (Office of Economics, U.S. International Trade Commission, January 1985), pp. 4–5. The U.S. study is cited above in note 2.

5. Jonathan D. Aronson and Peter F. Cowhey, *Trade in Services; A Case for Open Markets*, AEI Studies no. 415 (Washington, D.C.: American Enterprise Institute, 1984), p. 3.

6. Brock, *op.cit.*

7. U.S. International Trade Commission, *The Effects of Foreign Product Counterfeiting on U.S. Industry*, USITC Publication 1479 (January, 1984).

8. U.S. House of Representatives, Committee on Energy and Commerce, Subcommittee on Oversight and Investigation. *Unfair Foreign Trade Practices; Criminal Components of America's Trade Problem.* 99th Congress, 1st Session, Committee Print 99-H (1985), p. 5.

9. For the classic study of U.S. trade negotiations through the early twentieth century, see U.S. Tariff Commission, *Reciprocity and Commercial Treaties* (Washington, D.C.: U.S. Government Printing Office, 1919).

10. A few so-called "argol agreements" were negotiated under the authority of the Tariff Act of 1897. These provided for reciprocal duty reductions in argols, wines and sugar. All agreements except one with Cuba were terminated by the United States in 1909. See U.S. Tariff Commission, *op.cit.*, pp. 30–31.

11. U.S. Tariff Commission, *op.cit.*, p. 10.

12. Senator Robert Dole, "Reciprocity in Trade," *New York Times*, January 22, 1982, p. A31.

13. Leonard Weiss, "Reciprocity," in Seymour J. Rubin and Thomas R. Graham, eds., *Managing Trade Relations in the 1980s; Issues Involved in the GATT Ministerial Meeting of 1982* (Totowa, N.J.: Rowman & Allanheld, 1983), p. 179.

14. Under the TTA amendments, the consultations may be delayed.

15. The "fast track" is described in detail in chapter 3.

16. U.S. Senate Report No.249, 96th Congress, 1st Session (1979), as cited in Bart S. Fisher, "Section 301 of the Trade Act of 1974: Protection for U.S. Exporters of Goods, Services, and Capital," *Law and Policy in International Business*, 14, No.3 (1982): 597.

17. See the testimony of Ambassador William Brock, in U.S. House of Representatives, Committee on Ways and Means, *Market Expansion for U.S.-Produced Wine*. 98th Congress, 2nd session, Serial 98-96 (1985), pp. 23-24.

18. Office of the U.S. Trade Representative, *Annual Report on National Trade Estimates* (Washington, D.C.: USTR, October 1985), p. 1.

19. Office of the U.S. Trade Representative, "Administration Releases Trade Barriers Report," press release of October 30, 1985.

20. For a description of the structure and responsibilities of the advisory committees, see Office of the U.S. Trade Representative, *Annual Report to the President of the United States on the Trade Agreements Program, Twenty-Seventh Issue* (Washington, D.C.: USTR, 1984), pp. 127-128.

21. The actual retaliation did not fall into place until November 1, 1985, as both sides had hoped to reach a negotiated settlement before that date.

3
Bilateral Negotiating Authority

T itle IV of the Trade and Tariff Act of 1984 specifically provides the president with the authority to conclude a reciprocal free trade agreement (FTA) with Israel. It also establishes expedited congressional procedures for the ratification of such an agreement. The authority of this title can also be used to negotiate bilateral tariff agreements with other unspecified countries. Canada and other countries may request negotiations under this authority, but no such requests have been made as of this writing, and the Congress retains the right to disapprove any negotiations or agreements.

Genesis of the U.S.–Israeli FTA

As a small country with few natural resources, Israel is particularly dependent on foreign trade. The nation has enjoyed preferential trade relations with the United States and other industrialized countries for over a decade, being a beneficiary developing country of the Generalized System of Preferences (GSP). Prior to the renewal of the GSP in 1984 (see chapter 4), however, the future of the program was in doubt. Furthermore, the potential value of the GSP was limited by the program's exclusions of various products of interest to Israel, either because the product was not designated for the GSP or because it was excluded by the program's built-in safeguards against excessive import penetration. For these reasons, as well as for political considerations, Israel hoped to negotiate a more comprehensive and secure trading relationship with the United States.

The government of Israel first proposed the idea of a free trade area with the United States in 1981. Free trade areas are a deviation from the GATT principles of nondiscriminatory, most-favored-nation (MFN) treatment, but are allowed under GATT article XXIV when certain conditions are fulfilled.[1] Israel already benefited from such an arrangement with the European Community.[2] The Reagan administration responded favorably to the proposal and initially explored the possibilities of a companion arrangement with Egypt. The Egyptian government did not accept this idea, however, and no progress was made for nearly two years. Israel renewed its request for bilateral discussions in 1983, and was rewarded by a joint statement from President Reagan and Prime Minister Shamir on November 29, 1983, calling for the negotiation of a bilateral free trade area.

The United States began formal negotiations with Israel in January 1984, while concurrently discussing the necessary authority with the House Ways and Means Committee and the Senate Finance Committee.[3] Most members of the congressional trade committees welcomed the proposal from the start, but their enthusiasm stemmed more from political support for Israel than from a penchant for bilateral trade agreements. Some members of Congress and several domestic groups registered caution. First, certain congressmen were concerned about the extent of the authority the administration sought. The executive branch might conceivably use an FTA authority as an indirect means of entering a new MTN round, without first receiving the express approval of the Congress. The USTR responded to this concern by pledging that the administration would not use the authority for any purpose other than bilateral agreements with Israel and perhaps a few other trading partners.[4]

Second, some groups objected to the precedent that the FTA would set as well as the U.S. obligations under the GATT to extend similar treatment to other nations. The AFL–CIO and the textile and apparel industry were worried by the implications of the FTA, and feared that similar negotiations might be undertaken with the European Community, South Korea, and the Philippines.[5] The AFL–CIO was also concerned about the possible inconsistencies of the FTA proposal with the bilateral and multilateral obligations of the United States. The union spokesmen pointed out that the proposal represented a deviation from the MFN treatment required by the GATT, and noted the MFN clauses contained in the bilateral treaties of friendship, commerce and navigation (FCN) between the United States and forty-eight of its trading partners. The MFN obligations of the GATT and the FCN treaties might require that any tariff concessions extended to Israel be granted to most other U.S. trading partners.[6]

Administration spokesmen did not fully dispel concerns over the potential application of the FTA authority when they stated that, while their immediate goal was to negotiate an FTA with Israel, they also desired the discretionary power to reach similar agreements with other U.S. trading partners.[7] Chairman Gibbons of the Trade Subcommittee and some other members applauded this initiative, but the Congress still intended to keep any future negotiations within the bounds of congressional oversight.[8]

Third, many groups were concerned over the product coverage of the proposed FTA. Unlike the Generalized System of Preferences and the Caribbean Basin Initiative, both of which exclude textiles, footwear, and other sensitive products, the FTA proposal would include all products traded between the two countries. The administration was adamant upon this point, insisting that any product exclusions would be inconsistent with U.S. obligations under the GATT. Article XXIV of the GATT requires that free trade areas cover "substantially all trade" among their parties. Product exclusions in the FTA would invite challenges to the legality of the arrangement. The administration was also concerned by the snowball effect that any product exclusions would have: excluding one industry from the scheme would make it more difficult to deny the requests of others.

Several domestic industries feared that an FTA would attract new and unfettered import competition from Israel. Many represented agricultural producers from California, whose Mediterranean climate produces the same crops exported by Israel, such as tomatoes, avocados, roses, garlic, onions, and olives. The congressional committees also heard objections from domestic producers of textiles, leather goods, footwear, jewelry, bromine, medical diagnostic equipment, and sporting arms.[9] While nearly all of these industries professed their support for Israel and the proposed FTA, they requested that their own industry be protected from unbridled import competition.[10] These industries were unsuccessful in limiting the product coverage of the FTA, but may have influenced the decision to phase in duty reductions on some of their products on an extended schedule.

The Congress approved the administration's proposal for an FTA authority, but the concerns raised in the hearings led it to amend the proposal in several respects. These will now be described.

How the FTA Mechanism Works

The administration's plan for authorizing FTA negotiations centered on amending the nontariff barrier (NTB) authority of the Trade Act of 1974. The direct tariff-cutting authority of the 1974 Act expired in 1982, but section 102(b) still conferred authority to negotiate agreements on NTBs. The president may:

> enter into trade agreements with foreign countries or instrumentalities providing for the harmonization, reduction, or elimination of such barriers (or other distortions) or providing for the prohibition of or limitations on the imposition of such barriers (or other distortions).

This authority was used by the United States to ratify the various Tokyo Round NTB codes, and may also be used to approve a new safeguards code if and when it is drafted in the GATT.[11] The authority would have expired in 1980, but in 1979, the Congress extended the life of section 102(b) through January 3, 1988.

Any agreements that are reached under this section are subject to a special fast-track approval by Congress. The president must notify both the House and the Senate of intentions to submit implementing legislation on the fast track no less than ninety days before entering into an agreement, and must submit a draft implementing bill shortly after the agreement is reached. These bills are not subject to amendment, and must be approved or rejected by the Congress within sixty days of receipt. In this way, the section 102(b) authority plots a shortcut through the normal congressional ratification procedure, and places greater authority in the hands of the executive branch and the trade committees.

The Reagan administration requested that the Congress allow it to submit FTA agreements on tariffs for fast-track approval. This would give the executive branch an agile means of negotiating and submitting trade agreements for ratification, while still assuring that the Congress could influence the content of these agreements. The TTA explicitly grants the authority for fast-track approval of an FTA with Israel, but the trade committees of the Congress reserved the right to approve or disapprove future negotiations with other parties. In order to negotiate bilateral agreements with countries other than Israel, the executive branch must notify and consult with the House Ways and Means Committee and the Senate Finance Committee at least sixty legislative days before it submits its ninety-day notice of an impending agreement. Either committee can veto the proposal if it chooses. The TTA ensures that the benefits extended to Israel in an FTA will not be automatically extended to other countries through the MFN principle. An amendment to section 102(b) provides that:

> Notwithstanding any other provision of law, no trade benefit shall be extended to any country by reason of the extension of any trade benefit to another country under a trade agreement entered into under [this authority] with such other country.

This somewhat convoluted language effectively precludes the application of duty-free privileges to other countries through the MFN principle or through bilateral FCN treaties. Concessions negotiated under this proviso may conceivably be in violation of U.S. international obligations, at least under the FCN treaties, but there have been no challenges arising from such a claim thus far.

The stipulation against MFN extension is a radical departure not only from article I of the GATT, but also from the conditional MFN approach taken during the nineteenth century. Neither the TTA nor the U.S.–Israeli FTA provide that other countries may receive the benefits accorded by this arrangement upon extending similar concessions to the United States.

Provisions of the U.S.–Israeli FTA

The United States and Israel negotiated the FTA between January 1984 and March 1985, and formally signed the agreement on April 22, 1985. The U.S.

Congress gave its approval via the fast-track, and President Reagan signed the implementing legislation on June 11. Israel ratified the agreement on August 18. The first stage of tariff reductions came into effect on September 1.

Phased-in Implementation

Rather than exclude some products entirely from the FTA, which might imperil its legitimacy within the GATT system, U.S. and Israeli negotiators agreed to phase sensitive products in more slowly than others. Several products deemed to be sensitive were among those identified in the congressional hearings, but the chief guidance given for U.S. trade negotiators came from the U.S. International Trade Commission. A confidential USITC report to the USTR indicated which products would be most sensitive, and therefore required a longer period of adjustment to import competition.

The agreement establishes four classes of goods for each country, together with stepped stages of implementation. The value of trade covered in each class in indicated in table 3–1. In the first stage, all products that are not subject to the special stages are entirely duty-free as of September 1, 1985. In 1982, these products amounted to $414.7 million of all U.S. imports from Israel (80.5 percent), and $670.8 million in Israeli imports from the United States (52.5 percent). The second- and third-stage products are somewhat sensitive, and will be phased in gradually over a period of several years.

The fourth-stage products are those that each party considered to be the most import-sensitive. No duty reductions will be made in this freeze category until 1990, but all of these goods will be entirely duty-free in 1995. (In the case of U.S. imports from Israel, however, 64.8 percent of these most sensitive products are already eligible for duty-free treatment under the GSP). Under the advice of the USITC, the products that the United States placed on its sensitive

Table 3–1
Staged Duty Reductions in the U.S.–Israeli Free Trade Area
(in terms of 1982 trade, in $ thousands and percentage of total imports)

Stage	U.S. Imports from Israel		Israeli Imports from the United States	
	Value	Share	Value	Share
I	$414.7	80.5%	$670.8	52.5%
II	27.8	5.4	402.8	31.5
III	4.7	0.9	39.5	3.1
IV	67.9	13.2	164.4	12.9
Total	$515.1	100.0	$1,277.5	100.0

Source: Statement of Doral S. Cooper, Assistant U.S. Trade Representative, before the House Ways and Means Committee, March 6, 1985.

list include leather goods, footwear, gold necklaces, certain bromide products, cut roses, olives, citrus juices, and dehydrated garlic. For its part, Israel placed on its list U.S. exports of refrigerators, radio navigation equipment, aluminum bars, certain dairy products, dates, apples, and grapes.

The implementation schedule negotiated in the FTA constitutes a minimum timetable for compliance. Either party can step up its implementation of the liberalization schedules if it so chooses; this could offer room for possible give and take in the future.

Textile Imports

Although the FTA will eventually eliminate all duties on textile and apparel products, there remained some question as to this action's effect on the textile quota system. U.S. textile imports from nearly all countries outside of Europe are governed by the Multi Fiber Arrangement, which is a restrictive exception to the liberal trade rules of the GATT. The United States has negotiated bilateral textile restraint agreements under the auspices of the MFA with twenty-two supplier nations. A bilateral textile agreement with Israel had lapsed, due to lack of trade.

At the insistence of the U.S. textile lobby, U.S. trade negotiators insisted in congressional hearings that the FTA would not supercede the MFA. Israeli negotiators subsequently argued that because the MFA is a subsidiary agreement within the GATT system, and the FTA supercedes the GATT, then the FTA must logically supercede the MFA as well. The issue was resolved when an independent bilateral agreement on textiles was negotiated in November 1985, under which growth limits were set for U.S. imports of Israeli apparel, yarn, fabric, and textiles.

Rules of Origin

The FTA will only apply to products that meet its rules of origin, which are modeled after those of the Caribbean Basin Initiative:

1. Products must be imported directly from Israel into the customs territory of the United States.
2. Israeli products benefiting from the duty-free status must be grown, produced, or manufactured in Israel.
3. A minimum of 35 percent of the appraised value of the imported article must consist of the cost or value of the materials or direct processing costs incurred in Israel, and up to 15 percentage points of this 35 percent may consist of U.S. materials.
4. Products must undergo substantial transformation into a different article of commerce, and assembled products must undergo complex rather than simple assembly processes.

The 15–percent allowance imbedded within the 35–percent local content rule is identical to a provision in the one-way FTA of the Caribbean Basin Initiative (CBI). The purpose of this shared-content clause is to encourage U.S.–Israeli coproduction. In this way, the FTA rules of origin are more flexible than those of the GSP, and could mean duty-free treatment for some articles that had not previously qualified for the GSP.

Safeguards

The FTA does not directly alter the operation of U.S. antisubsidy or antidumping laws as they relate to Israel, although a separate agreement to phase out Israeli subsidies will result in Israel receiving an injury test. The terms of the FTA will allow Israel to be exempt in some cases from escape-clause actions of the United States. Article 5 specifies that:

> When, in the view of the importing Party, the importation of a product from the other Party is not a substantial cause of the serious injury or threat thereof . . . the importing Party may except the product of the other Party from any import relief that may be imposed with respect to imports of that product from third countries.

In effect, this means that the USITC may recommend to the president that Israel not be subject to import restrictions imposed under the escape clause *if* the commission finds that Israeli products do not contribute to the injury suffered by U.S. firms. This provision is roughly parallel to an exemption provided for CBI beneficiary countries in the Caribbean Basin Economic Recovery Act (except that it covers tariff and quota relief, whereas the CBI rule may only be applicable to tariff relief).

The legislation allows for fast-track removal of certain agricultural products from duty-free treatment in emergencies. Both parties can maintain quantitative restrictions on agricultural goods or apply temporary trade restrictions for balance of payments reasons. Furthermore, Israel may continue to impose duties until 1991 on certain products in order to protect infant industries, and has the right (subject to the principle of national treatment) to exclude products that violate the nation's dietary laws.

Services, Intellectual Property Rights, and Performance Requirements

Perhaps the most interesting aspects of the FTA are the special provisions covering the new issues of interest to the United States (see chapter 2). A Declaration on Trade in Services that accompanies the agreement is the first trade agreement ever to cover the full range of trade in services, and U.S.

negotiators hope that it will set a precedent for possible future agreements with other nations. The nonbinding declaration establishes the intention of both parties to "endeavor to achieve open market access for trade in services with the other nation" and "to assure that trade in services with the other nation is governed by the principle of national treatment." Israel and the United States have agreed to continue discussion on services trade under the FTA umbrella. This might possibly lead to a binding agreement on the matter.

Article 14 of the agreement addresses the U.S. objectives in intellectual property rights by declaring that "nationals and companies of each Party shall continue to be accorded national and most favored nation treatment with respect to obtaining, maintaining and enforcing" patents, copyrights, and trademarks.

The agreement deals tangentially with trade-related investment issues, which are already the subject of the existing bilateral Treaty of Friendship, Commerce and Navigation (FCN). The FCN treaty guarantees equal treatment under the law for domestic and foreign investments, and provides that expropriation will only take place for public purposes and with compensation. Article 13 of the FTA clarifies the coverage of the FCN concerning trade-related performance requirements by stating that "neither Party shall impose, as a condition of establishment . . . requirements to export any amount of production resulting from such investments or to purchase locally-produced goods and services."

Israeli Subsidies and the Injury Test

As a further condition of the FTA, Israel agreed to freeze its existing subsidies, phase them out over a period of no longer than six years, and sign the GATT Subsidies Code no later than the effective date of the agreement. The commitment was made in a nonbinding letter from Minister Ariel Sharon to U.S. Trade Representative Brock. In exchange for adhering to the Subsidies Code and agreeing to phase out subsidies, Israel will receive an injury test from the United States in any future countervailing duty cases.

Significance of the FTA Authority

The U.S.–Israeli FTA is of limited economic significance for the United States. U.S. imports from Israel in 1984 amounted to only $1.8 billion, accounting for just 0.5 percent of total U.S. imports. The real importance of the FTA authority lies in the precedent that it could set for similar agreements with other countries.

The expanded section 102(b) authority may be used through January 3, 1988 to negotiate bilateral agreements with other U.S. trading partners. This provision does not restrict the products that may be discussed, the countries with which negotiations might be conducted, or the degree to which tariffs might be reduced. It appears that the executive branch can use this authority in any bilateral negotiation to reduce, harmonize, or eliminate any duty, provided that the congressional trade committees do not turn down the administration's proposals. However, Congress only contemplated free trade and sectoral agreements when considering this authority, and the Reagan administration specifically ruled out its use as a proxy authority to enter any new MTN round.

No formal requests have been made of the Congress to allow the executive branch to enter into bilateral negotiations, although Canada may be given serious consideration and the member states of the Association of South East Asian Nations (ASEAN) are also possible candidates. The United States and Canada have attempted to establish a special bilateral trade regime many times over the past two centuries, and succeeded from 1855 to 1866. The two nations have subscribed to a sectoral agreement covering trade in automobiles since 1965, and have recently discussed the possibility of negotiating arrangements covering steel, informatics, government procurement, mass transit, and agricultural equipment. The Reagan administration requested in 1984 that the FTA authority explicitly cover a possible agreement with Canada, and the Congress seemed intent upon approving this request. The Trudeau government fell just prior to the passage of the TTA, however, and the Congress considered it imprudent to include such a provision until the new Mulroney government clarified its trade policy. As of this writing, Ottawa and Washington appear close to initiating negotiations for a Comprehensive Trade Agreement (CTA), but no formal request has yet been transmitted to Capitol Hill.

A U.S.–Canadian agreement would certainly be of far greater economic consequence than the U.S.–Israeli FTA even if not all sectors or products were covered; bilateral trade with Canada reached $110.8 billion in 1984, making Canada the largest U.S. trading partner. U.S.–Canadian trade, in fact, accounts for the single greatest bilateral flow of goods in the world. Canadian trade relations with the United States involve contentious issues, such as the allegation that Canadian timber prices constitute a natural resource subsidy. If negotiations for a CTA with Canada do get underway, the debate on Capitol Hill will be much more intense than it was for the Israeli FTA.

It is also possible that the United States would use its FTA authority to negotiate an agreement with the ASEAN. U.S. negotiators would like to ensure that the ASEAN markets are not dominated entirely by Japan, while the ASEAN countries hope to improve their access to the U.S. market. The technical difficulties posed by such a negotiation, however, would be enormous. The ASEAN member countries impose widely differing levels of market protection, and have disparate economic interests. Many members of Congress are concerned over the competitive strength of these countries, and would heartily resist any proposals that would increase their access to the U.S. market.

At bottom, the real question is whether the United States will opt for discriminatory, bilateral agreements as a model for future liberalization, or if it will pursue multilateral and nondiscriminatory liberalization in the GATT. Free trade purists tend to look upon the U.S.–Israeli FTA with alarm. Veteran trade observer Sidney Weintraub views the FTA as "a potentially more significant departure from globalism and non-discrimination than any previous action since World War II," and concludes that "the United States is no longer a missionary for principle."[12]

The Reagan administration's adherence to multilateralism definitely changed over the course of five years. The trade policy white paper of 1981 warned against the dangers of "creeping bilateralism,"[13] but the September 1985 white paper stated that "the United States is interested in the possibility of achieving further liberalization of trade and investment through the negotiation of bilateral free-trade arrangements such as the one recently concluded with Israel."[14] The administration's view in 1985 is that bilateral or regional negotiations are not necessarily a substitute for multilateral negotiations, but that "such agreements could complement our multilateral efforts and facilitate a higher degree of liberalization, mutually beneficial to both parties, than would be possible within the multilateral context."[15] Bilateral negotiations might therefore run concurrently with multilateral discussions.

Notes

1. Article XXIV permits the establishment of free trade areas or customs unions if the agreement eliminates duties and other restrictive measures on "substantially all" trade between the parties within a reasonable period of time, and the duties and other regulations of commerce maintained by the parties are not higher or more restrictive to the trade of third parties than the countries had in place prior to the agreement. Waivers may be sought in the GATT for FTA proposals that do not meet these requirements.

2. Under the terms of the EC–Israeli FTA, the EC granted Israel duty-free treatment for most industrial products after July 1, 1977. The EC delayed full concessions on certain sensitive products until December 31, 1979. In return, Israel established a five-stage process for eliminating its duties on about 60 percent of its imports from the EC; the full package was in effect as of January 1, 1980. The remainder of Israel's imports from the EC were to be granted duty–free treatment by 1985, with two possible two-year extensions if requested by Israel. Both extensions have been requested.

3. Transcripts of the hearings on this matter, together with submissions by the administration and private witnesses, can be found in the following congressional documents:

United States Senate, Committee on Finance, Subcommittee on International Trade, *Proposal for Free-Trade Area With Israel.* 98th Congress, 2nd session,

Senate Hearing, 98–900 (February 6, 1984) (hereinafter cited as *Senate Hearings*).

United States House of Representatives, Committee on Ways and Means, Subcommittee on Trade, *Proposed United States-Israel Free Trade Area*. 98th Congress, 2nd session, Serial 98–72 (May 22, June 13–14, 1984) (hereinafter cited as *House Hearings*).

4. Written responses of the USTR to questions submitted by the Senate Finance Committee, in *Senate Hearings*, pp. 22–25.

5. See the testimony of the American Fiber/Textile/Apparel Coalition in *Senate Hearings*, pp. 141–145, and the testimony of the AFL–CIO in *House Hearings*, pp. 109–115. The specific references to the EC, the Philippines, and South Korea were made by the AFL–CIO.

6. See *House Hearings*, pp. 114–115, for a list of the forty-eight FCN treaties between the United States and other countries.

7. The USTR stated that:

The Administration is seeking broader tariff authority than simply limited to the establishment of a U.S.-Israel FTA. It is our belief that the President could use this authority to conclude highly advantageous and GATT-consistent arrangements with selected trading partners to promote freer trade on a bilateral basis. (See *Senate Hearings*, pp. 22–23.)

8. Chairman Gibbons stated:

I want to tell everyone that I will be happy to introduce a bill that does the same thing for . . . any other nation that wants to enter into that kind of negotiation with the United States. (See *House Hearings*, p. 4.)

9. See both *Senate Hearings* and *House Hearings* for the testimony of these groups.

10. The textile and apparel industry was unique in this respect. Representatives of this industry not only requested that their products be exempt from the coverage of the FTA, but also that the United States not enter into the agreement to begin with. See *Senate Hearings*, pp. 141–115.

11. Some members of Congress were concerned that negotiating on specific products prior to the granting of authority from Congress or receipt of product advice from the U.S. International Trade Commission might be improper. The USTR responded that no specific products would be discussed until advice was received from the USITC, and that all other procedural requirements (including consultations with the Congress) laid out by the Trade Act of 1974 were being followed. See *Senate Hearings*, pp. 22.

12. Weintraub provides a trenchant criticism of the numerous departures from nondiscriminatory trade, including the north–south departures (GSP, the Caribbean Basin Initiative and the Lome agreements between the European Community and the African, Caribbean, and Pacific countries), the east–west departure (denial of MFN treatment for most Soviet-bloc countries), and the west–west departure (special dispensation for the EC's common market). Weintraub views the gradual U.S. acceptance and even promotion of discriminatory trade regimes as a product and symptom of the diminishing leadership of the United States in the global trading system. See "Selective Trade Liberalization and Restriction" in Ernest H. Preeg, ed., *Hard Bargaining Ahead: U.S. Trade Policy and Developing Countries*, U.S.-Third World Policy Perspectives no. 4 (Washington, D.C.: Overseas Development Council, 1985).

13. See Brock, cited in note 8 of chapter 1. The reference in this instance was to special bilateral commodity arrangements.

14. Office of the U.S. Trade Representative, "Administration Statement on International Trade Policy" (September 23, 1985), p. 12.

15. *Ibid.*, p. 13.

4

Renewal of the Generalized System of Preferences: Neoreciprocity and the Newly Industrialized Countries

The U.S. GSP is a decade-old program that provides duty-free access to the U.S. market for eligible exports from most developing countries. The program was originally proposed in the United Nations Conference on Trade and Development (UNCTAD) in the 1960s, where it was argued that private enterprise (trade) rather than government intervention (aid) is the most secure and fair means of encouraging economic development in third world countries. The GSP programs sponsored by the industrialized countries offer developing nations a margin of tariff preference in their access to advanced markets.

The original GSP authority was granted by of the Trade Act of 1974, and was due to expire in January 1985 if it was not renewed by the Congress. Despite concerns that the program would be eliminated or gutted by the 98th Congress, the GSP was reauthorized without crippling changes. Proposals were made to limit the program, but few were included in the new law. No countries are directly graduated (that is, eliminated from the program) by name, and no currently eligible products were eliminated from the program's coverage.

The renewed GSP is, however, notably different from the original program in one fundamental respect. The program now includes an element of reciprocity that could restrict benefits for some countries and liberalize them for others. The new negotiability of the GSP will be of greatest importance to the most advanced beneficiary countries. While the GSP does not constitute an explicit negotiating authority for the executive branch, it may become an important tool.

The GSP before 1984

The GSP is the single most significant manifestation of the principle of special and differential treatment for developing countries. Even so, the program is only a modest and limited concession to third-world demand for "new international economic order."

The idea of creating a preferential trading regime for the benefit of developing countries is at least as old as the ill-starred International Trade Organization (ITO) charter negotiated in Havana in 1946. Although the ITO charter provided that "new preferences could be granted in the interests of economic development," the temporary GATT made no such provision.[1] The notion of special treatment languished until the early 1960s. Developing countries began pressing for tariff preferences in 1964 during the first U.N. Conference on Trade and Development. In 1968 at the second conference they obtained a commitment in principle from the developed countries, leading in 1971 to the "Agreed Conclusions" of a special UNCTAD committee. The committee determined that the preferences would be exclusively extended to the developing states and territories, and that no third country could demand access to these preferences by invoking most-favored-nation (MFN) treatment. In the GATT, however, non-discrimination and the MFN principle militated against the adoption of any preferences. This required unanimous consent to waive article I of the GATT (the MFN clause), a special exemption that was later made permanent through an enabling clause negotiated in the Tokyo Round.[2]

The U.S. legislation authorizing the GSP was passed by the Congress as part of the Trade Act of 1974, which was not actually signed into law until early 1975. Nearly all developing countries were designated by President Ford as beneficiary developing countries (BDCs) by the time the U.S. GSP program became operational on January 1, 1976. The 1974 act provided that the program would expire on January 3, 1985, unless first renewed by the Congress.

Limited Effectiveness of the GSP

In the ensuing decade, the program failed to live up to the expectations raised in UNCTAD. Actual trade flows under the program are much lower than had been expected. In 1984, the United States imported $13.0 billion worth of products under the system, accounting for just 12.3 percent of all products imported from eligible developing countries, and 4.1 percent of U.S. imports from all sources. Analysts in the U.S. International Trade Commission estimate that GSP imports provide only about one-half of 1 percent of all products consumed in the United States.[3]

Moreover, the program's importance is limited by the low rate of U.S. tariffs (see table 1–1). The very same Trade Act of 1974 that established the GSP also provided the executive branch with the authority to bargain down U.S. tariffs in the Tokyo Round negotiations, thus eroding the margins of preference that the GSP offers to developing countries.[4] A program that is based entirely on tariff exonerations can only be effective for those products that face meaningful tariff barriers. When the Tokyo round tariff reductions are fully implemented in 1987, 31.0 percent of all raw materials and industrial products imported into the United States will be duty-free for countries that receive MFN treatment, and only 7.1 percent will be subject to duty rates in excess of 10 percent.[5]

Product Exclusions. The GSP excludes several important products from its coverage. Although developing countries had wanted the GSP to cover all of their exports to the industrialized countries, sponsoring countries restrict products that are felt to be sensitive to import competition. These restrictions either take the form of GSP quotas (as are applied by some European countries) or outright exclusions from GSP eligibility. In the case of the United States, only those products that are explicitly designated for GSP eligibility in the Tariff Schedules of the United States (TSUS) can actually enter duty-free under the program.[6] These designations are made by the president, acting on the advice of the USTR.

The Trade Act of 1974 enumerated several products that the president is not allowed to designate for the GSP, including textile and apparel articles subject to textile agreements, watches, most footwear, and import-sensitive electronic, steel, and glass products, as well as any other articles that it determines to be "import-sensitive in the context of the Generalized System of Preferences."[7] Many of these excluded articles are labor-intensive consumer goods in which low-wage developing countries have a clear comparative advantage. By excluding them from GSP eligibility, the Congress severely limited the program's coverage.[8]

President Ford designated 2,729 articles as eligible for the GSP in 1976. With some products added and a few removed in subsequent years, the number gradually rose to 3,054 in 1984, or about one-third of the approximately 9,000 articles in the TSUS. In other words, one-third of all TSUS items are dutiable and eligible for the GSP, another third are already duty-free for all countries receiving MFN treatment, and the remaining third are dutiable and ineligible for the GSP. During 1984, the eligible items accounted for only 28.2 percent of all U.S. imports (both dutiable and nondutiable) from the beneficiary countries.[9] For the middle-income GSP beneficiaries—the great majority of the developing countries—the figure was just 11.6 percent.[10] In terms of product categories, 26 percent of general manufactures were ineligible for the GSP as of 1982, as were 52 percent of chemicals, 58 percent of machinery and equipment, 72 percent of minerals and metals, 73 percent of agricultural products, 84 percent of forest products, and 94 percent of textiles and apparel.[11]

Safeguards. The GSP is further limited by several built-in safeguards. The rationale behind the safeguards is to ensure that GSP benefits go to those countries that can gain the most from them. When beneficiary countries become economically competitive in a product, they no longer need a margin of preference. By removing a competitive developing country from GSP eligibility, the benefits may then be enjoyed by other beneficiary countries that still need a boost. U.S. Trade Representative Brock argued that, "It is economically illogical, not to mention unfair, to give the same degree of tariff preferences to the advanced developing countries of East Asia as to the countries of the Sahel."[12] Critics argue that the real intent and effect of the safeguards are to protect domestic industries from import competition. There is little empirical support for the claim that safeguards work to the benefit of lesser developed countries. A USITC study concluded that the countries which benefit the most from GSP exclusions are industrialized countries and the advanced developing countries that are not excluded.[13]

The single most restrictive safeguard is the "competitive-need limit" (CNL) that places a cap on the quantity of any one good that a BDC can import duty-free into the United States under the program. The CNL provides that in most cases a country will lose its GSP eligibility for any product in the year following one in which its imports into the United States exceed the competitive-need limits.[14] These limits are set at 50 percent of the value of total U.S. imports or a quantitative limit adjusted annually to reflect growth in the U.S. GNP. The figure was originally set at $25 million in 1975, and rose to $63.8 million by 1984. If a country's exports subsequently drop below the competitive-need limits, the product can be redesignated for the program. Exceptions are made for products that were not produced in the United States as of January 1985, or—as is discussed shortly—for products that enter at a *de minimis* level.

The CNL limits have a definite and intentional bias toward curtailing GSP eligibility for the arger and more sophisticated developing country exporters, such as Brazil, Hong Kong, Israel, Mexico, Singapore, South Korea, and Taiwan. These nations, frequently called *newly industrialized countries* (NICs), have been among the true success stories in the third world.[15] By gaining appreciable shares of import markets, however, they have also earned the ire of their competitors in the industrialized countries. As seen in table 4–1, the advanced beneficiary countries accounted for 74.1 percent of all U.S. imports under the GSP in 1984, but also tallied up 93.8 percent of all competitive-need eliminations imposed by the United States that year.

Even with these competitive-need limitations, however, the NICs have fared much better under the GSP than have the low- or middle-income LDCs. Fifteen percent of all imports from the advanced beneficiary countries entered duty-free under the GSP in 1984, compared to 7.7 percent from the middle-income countries and 10.4 percent from the low-income countries. In answer to requests from domestic industries, therefore, the automatic eligibility removals of the CNL were supplemented over the years by various graduation mechanisms to further limit the benefits that the NICs receive under the GSP. These additional safeguards have been used with increasing frequency since 1981.

Table 4-1
U.S. Imports for Consumption from GSP Beneficiary Countries, by Country Group, 1984
(in $ millions, customs value basis)

	Advanced Beneficiaries[a]	Middle-Income Beneficiaries[b]	Low-Income Beneficiaries[c]
Total U.S. imports	$62,591.4	$42,482.4	$870.5
Imports eligible for GSP	24,745.4	4,926.5	234.1
As a percentage of beneficiary group's total imports	39.5	11.6	26.9
Beneficiary group's percent share of total GSP-eligible imports	82.7	16.5	0.8
Imports excluded by competitive-need eliminations	12,286.4	780.9	32.9
As a percentage of beneficiary group's imports eligible for GSP	49.7	15.9	14.1
Beneficiary group's percent share of total competitive-need eliminations	93.8	6.0	0.3
Imports actually entering duty-free under GSP	9,629.5	3,275.7	90.6
As a percentage of beneficiary group's total imports	15.4	7.7	10.4
As a percentage of beneficiary group's imports eligible for GSP	38.9	66.5	38.7
Beneficiary group's percent share of total GSP imports	74.1	25.2	0.7

Source: Adapted from U.S. International Trade Commission, *Operation of the Trade Agreements Program*, 36th annual report, USITC publication 1725 (July, 1985) p. 219.

Note: Totals may exceed 100% due to rounding.

[a] Advanced beneficiary countries: Brazil, Hong Kong, Israel, South Korea, Mexico, Taiwan, and Singapore.

[b] Middle-income beneficiary countries: 107 BDCs not listed as either advanced or low-income.

[c] Low-income beneficiary countries: 26 countries designated as least-developed developing countries in headnote 3(d) of the TSUS (not the same as the 32 least-developed countries so designated by the president).

The USTR conducts an annual GSP review for CNL eliminations, during which new products may also be designated, previously eligible products may be removed from the GSP, *de minimis* waivers may be granted for products that exceed the 50-percent limit but not the dollar limit of the CNL, and products previously removed via the CNL may be redesignated for eligibility. While these mechanisms may be applied to imports from any or all GSP beneficiary countries, their chief purpose is to limit the GSP benefits for NICs.

As can be seen from table 4-2, exclusions under the CNL are the most important order of business in these reviews, followed by the redesignation of

Table 4-2

Results of the Annual GSP Reviews of U.S. Imports, 1981-1984

(in $ millions and percentages)[a]

	1981	1982	1983	1984
Imports under Competitive-Need Designations				
Value of exclusions in force	782	7,108	10,661	13,797
Imports of products eligible for redesignation	810	1,012	1,181	2,036
Imports of redesignated products	213	207	155	246
(percentage of total)	26.3	20.5	13.1	11.9
Imports of products not redesignated				
(Graduated products)	597	805	1,026	1,790
(percentage of total)	73.7	79.5	86.9	87.9
Product Eligibility				
New product designations	76	10	7	41
Product removals	n.a.	73	33	0
Country-specific product removals	54	95	183	163
Net Change[b]	n.a.	− 158	− 209	− 122
De Minimis Waivers				
Eligible products	43	49	54	313
Waivers granted	41	47	52	252
(percentage of eligible products)	95.3	95.9	96.3	80.5

Source: Calculated from information supplied by the U.S. Trade Representative GSP Information Center.

n.a. = not available.

[a] All values are expressed in terms of the total products which the rule would have affected in the review year.

[b] Because changes are denominated in terms of a previous year's trade data, which is a constantly changing base, the figures are only roughly indicative of trends.

products. If imports of a product excluded under the CNL drop below the competitive-need limits, the USTR may, at its discretion, redesignate the product for GSP eligibility. Redesignations are virtually automatic for low- and middle-income countries, but the USTR graduates many products imported from the NICs by refusing to redesignate them. The rate of graduation by means of nonredesignation has stepped up from $597 million in 1981 (73.7 percent of eligible products) to $1.8 billion in 1984 (87.9 percent of eligible products).

The USTR may make additional products eligible for the program, or remove them from eligibility on either a global or country-specific basis. These decisions are based primarily on petitions submitted to the USTR by foreign governments, domestic and foreign firms, and trade associations. The petitions from domestic industries requesting that a product be removed from GSP eligibility are roughly equivalent in motive, content, and effect to the trade-remedy petitions submitted by U.S. industries to the Department of Commerce and the U.S. International Trade Commission (see part II). The standards of proof applied by the USTR in the annual review are much less formal than those employed in the trade-remedy proceedings.

More TSUS items are added to GSP eligibility than are removed in these reviews. Measured in terms of total trade values, however, the recent rate of new product designations is well below the combined rate of global and country-specific product removals. Nearly all of the specific product removals are applied to the NICs. Depending on one's perspective, this could either be taken as a sign that the GSP has helped the advanced beneficiary countries to gain a competitive edge, and that they no longer need its assistance, or that U.S. domestic industries have succeeded in curtailing GSP benefits for their foreign competitors.

The USTR may also grant *de minimis* waivers during the annual reviews. When the "50 percent of U.S. imports" portion of the CNL equation is exceeded, but imports amount to a *de minimis* level in absolute terms, the USTR may waive the CNL. (The 1983 *de minimis* level was $1.3 million; this increases each year to reflect growth in U.S. GNP.) It is the policy of the USTR to automatically grant *de minimis* waivers unless a domestic industry raises an objection. Until the most recent review (effective mid-1985), Mexico and Taiwan were the only countries that had been denied waivers on some products.

A final safeguard relates to the escape clause (see chapter 5). If the United States invokes the escape clause to restrict imports of any product, that product automatically loses GSP eligibility. This is done even if GSP imports of the product do not contribute to the injury of the U.S. industry. If the GSP imports are considered to be a cause of injury, the USITC may recommend GSP removal as one of the possible remedies.

Rules of Origin. The GSP lays out rules of origin for eligible imports. The purpose of these rules is to ensure that all goods benefiting from the program are bona fide products of the BDCs and have not simply passed through a developing country in order to receive duty-free treatment. To qualify for the GSP:

1. An import must be imported directly from a BDC into the customs territory of the United States.

2. No less than 35 percent of the direct cost of processing must originate in the BDC.

3. The import must undergo substantial transformation into a different article of commerce, with assembled items being the product of complex rather than simple assembly processes.

Developing countries often criticize the rules of origin for imposing significant costs in terms of documentation and administrative difficulties, and for establishing an arbitrary standard that excludes many assembled products. The rules do not distinguish between foreign inputs and inputs that were originally purchased in the United States.

Taken together, the low tariff rates, product exclusions, safeguards, and rules of origin have made the GSP program far less beneficial than had originally been hoped by some developing countries.[16] Despite these shortcomings, however, many beneficiary countries have come to view the program as a bellwether of north–south trade relations. The GSP is also a boon to a limited number of LDC exporters, multinational corporations, and U.S. importers that trade in those few products that would otherwise face significant tariff barriers.

The GSP Renewal Fight

As the foregoing analysis indicates, the beneficiary countries of the GSP have been frustrated by structural deficiencies in the program. Many of them saw the GSP renewal process as an opportunity to bring about real reforms. Developing countries suggested that ineligible products be brought under the GSP umbrella, the rules of origin be liberalized or even eliminated, and the graduation mechanisms be abolished.[17] They were joined in their efforts by some U.S. industries that benefit from the GSP program, while the U.S. Chamber of Commerce and other organizations suggested their own set of liberal reforms. One proposal supported by U.S. businesses would allow U.S. inputs to be counted toward the BDC's minimum 35 percent of direct cost of processing that is required by the rules of origin.[18]

As it turned out, however, GSP supporters were fortunate to have the program renewed at all. The political atmosphere of the 98th Congress was much different from that of the 93rd. The GSP has always been based on the twin considerations of aid to the developing countries and the pursuit of U.S. economic interests, but the balance seems to have tipped from the former to the latter between 1974 and 1984. The Reagan administration encouraged this shift by basing its arguments for GSP renewal on the enlightened self-interest of the United States. The testimony of Clayton Yeutter to the House Ways and Means Committee in 1983—two years before he was made the U.S. Trade Representative—may be considered representative of the general tone of the GSP renewal process:

> GSP need not, and should not, be considered a global welfare program on the part of the United States. I would rather evaluate it on the basis of "What's in it for us?" instead of "What's in it for them?" and, in doing so, I find ample reason to support its renewal. The United States has very likely benefited as much or more than the LDC recipients from the first nine years of this program.[19]

The future U.S. Trade Representative's sentiments were echoed by many other witnesses who noted that fully 40 percent of all U.S. exports are destined for the beneficiary countries and that U.S. purchases from these nations pave the way for expanded U.S. sales abroad. Still others were concerned that without the special access provided by the GSP, the debt crisis of the developing countries would be further aggravated.

Some interest groups hoped to multiply the U.S. returns from the GSP by using its trade preferences as a tool for extracting concessions from the beneficiary countries. The Trade Act of 1974 (as amended) had already provided a list of eligibility requirements that LDCs had to meet in order to be designated for the GSP, but these were almost never used to deny eligibility for countries that had already been designated as GSP beneficiaries. Nearly all LDCs with which the United States enjoys trade relations have received uninterrupted GSP treatment since 1976. The inauguration of President Reagan's Caribbean Basin Initiative (CBI), however, provided an instructive precedent in the utility of trade preferences as negotiating tools. The Caribbean Basin Economic Recovery Act of 1983 (the implementing legislation of the CBI) listed several designation criteria that U.S. negotiators employed to apply gentle pressure on several potential beneficiaries. This helped lead to agreements regarding expropriation disputes in Honduras and Panama, labor rights in Haiti, and intellectual property rights in Antigua, the Bahamas, and Jamaica. The United States also received assurances from several beneficiary countries that they would apply for membership in the GATT.

The CBI experience was repeated in the GSP renewal. The Reagan administration sold GSP renewal to the Congress by emphasizing its potential as a negotiating instrument, which assured the backing of several interest groups. The USTR wanted the authority to seek concessions from the NICs on U.S. access to their markets, as well as on other issues such as trade in services and trade-related investment rules. Groups that advocated stricter enforcement of intellectual property rights argued that GSP benefits should be contingent on a BDC's respect for the rights of U.S. authors and holders of trademarks, copyrights, and patents,[20] while unions and human rights organizations demanded that GSP treatment be made conditional on a country's respect for human rights and the development of free and independent labor unions.[21] The Reagan administration resisted only the last of these initiatives.

Some domestic interests consider the GSP to be a threat, and hoped that the Congress would either fail to renew the program, or would weaken it severely. Labor unions are probably the most implacable opponents of the GSP program, as they believe that U.S. workers have the least to gain and the most to lose from increased imports. The low wage scales prevailing in the third world make producers there highly competitive in labor-intensive products, and multinational corporations are tempted to move their operations from the United States to developing countries. In the view of organized labor, this means exporting U.S. jobs to the developing countries. The AFL–CIO convention passed a resolution in 1983 stating that:

> The Generalized System of Preferences should be repealed. At minimum, Congress must make import-sensitive items ineligible for GSP, limit its access to those countries that can realistically be considered developing nations, and exclude communist nations from the program.[22]

The AFL–CIO remained the most staunch opponent to GSP renewal in the 98th Congress. The union hoped to block renewal entirely or, failing that, to remove Hong Kong, South Korea, and Taiwan from eligibility. The AFL–CIO also supported proposals to make GSP benefits contingent upon a country's respect for human and trade union rights.

Some industries (including leather goods, steel products, and bicycles) joined the unions in urging the Congress to either terminate the program or exclude their own products from its coverage.[23] Rather than exclude any products or countries from the program by statute, however, the Congress opted for providing the executive branch with much broader administrative discretion. Depending on how this power is used, it could either make the program more or less liberal than it was prior to renewal.

The New Negotiability of the GSP

The White House had pressed the Congress for a full ten-year renewal of the program, without any statutory graduation of countries or products. The executive branch proposed fundamental alterations in the nature of the GSP, however, arguing that this was necessary both to win renewal of the program on Capitol Hill and to obtain U.S. negotiating objectives abroad. The Reagan proposal would make the GSP program walk the thin line between nonreciprocity (thus remaining consistent with the GATT enabling clause) and offering an inducement for beneficiary countries to open their markets and otherwise cooperate with the United States.

The renewal bill proposed by the administration—and subsequently passed by the Congress, with some changes—would make it easier for beneficiary developing nations to lose their GSP eligibility in some of their more competitive products, but it would also allow them to preserve or expand their GSP privileges through a new presidential waiver of the competitive-need limitations. This negotiating feature is primarily aimed at certain of the NICs. For this negotiable eligibility to work, the administration needed congressional approval on three points. First, the GSP program had to be kept intact, so that it would remain relatively attractive to the beneficiaries. Any irrevocable product or country graduations would decrease the usefulness of the program as a negotiating tool. Second, the administration needed the explicit authority to put more products in jeopardy of graduation, which would increase U.S. leverage.[24] Finally, the president needed the power to reward countries that offer trade concessions to the United States.

The mechanism for the new negotiability is the competitive need limits. Section 505 of the TTA directs the president to conduct a general review of GSP-eligible products no later than January 4, 1987, and periodically thereafter. The purpose of this review is to identify, on a country-specific basis, those products in which the beneficiary nations demonstrate ''a sufficient degree of competitiveness (relative to other beneficiary developing countries).'' Products that are deemed to be competitive will then be subject to a CNL that is roughly half of that which is applicable to all other products: $25 million or 25 percent of U.S. imports. The effect of this lower CNL will be to accelerate the graduation of these products. (It might be noted that the Trade Act of 1974 already gave the president the authority to reduce GSP benefits; the 1984 amendments make this a much more formal authority that enjoys the explicit approval of Capitol Hill.)

The law does not strictly define the conditions that make products competitive. In addition to examining purely economic considerations, the USTR will also take into account a BDC's willingness to liberalize its trade—particularly in products of interest to the United States. The threat of facing a lower CNL is intended to encourage NICs and other beneficiary countries to lower their tariff barriers and cooperate with the United States on other trade issues.

In addition to this stick, the legislation also provides the GSP program with a carrot. The carrot is a limited authority to waive the CNL altogether, provided that the president determines that it would be in the national economic interest to do so. Section 505 of the TTA directs the president to give great weight to the following factors in deciding whether or not to grant the waiver:

1. The extent to which the beneficiary developing country has assured the United States that such country will provide equitable and reasonable access to the markets and basic commodity resources of such country; and

2. The extent to which such country provides adequate and effective means under its laws for foreign nationals to secure, to exercise, and to enforce exclusive rights in intellectual property, including patent, trademark, and copyright rights.

In addition to these two factors, the president's decision on waivers is likely to be heavily influenced by the other issues raised in the review of the beneficiary country practices. This review will center on the degree to which the GSP beneficiary country fulfills the GSP designation requirements.

The president's waiver authority is circumscribed by the TTA in two ways. First, the chief executive must consult with the USITC on whether any industry in the United States is likely to be adversely affected by such a waiver. This requirement is standard; U.S. trade legislation requires the president to consult with the commission on the probable economic effects of nearly all actions that might affect the duty rates established in the tariff schedules. The president is only required to "receive the advice" of the USITC, however, and the commission is given no veto over the waivers.

Second, the TTA limits the total value of waivers that the president can grant to 30 percent of the value of all GSP imports in the previous calendar year.[25] Within this global limit of 30 percent, up to 15 percentage points may be allocated for the more advanced beneficiary countries. Several BDCs fit the criteria laid out by the TTA for "advanced" countries, but only Hong Kong, South Korea, Singapore, and Taiwan are likely to be affected by this provision.[26] Although these limits put a theoretical ceiling on the waiver authority, the president could still redesignate many GSP products that have been excluded through the CNL or that are in imminent danger of surpassing the limits. The USTR has calculated that—if the so-called "waiver pool" were to be based on 1984 GSP data—a total of $3.9 billion worth of waivers could be granted. The total value of waiver requests received by the USTR exceeds this figure by 19 percent. Within the subgroup of advanced BDCs, however, the total value of waiver requests is 63 percent over the allowable figure. These figures are based on the assumption that waivers would be granted in a given product only to the countries that requested them. The number of waiver requests that may be granted would be cut sharply if the USTR decides to extend the waivers on a nondiscriminatory basis to all GSP countries, rather than to just the country that requested the waiver. If this were the basis for calculation, then the requests received from all quarters would exceed the allowable figure by 69 percent, and the requests for the advanced BDCs would be 130 percent above the maximum.

The TTA makes two other changes in the operation of the competitive-need clause. The least-developed beneficiary countries are now entirely exempt from the CNL, and need only be designated by the president (and not rejected by the Congress) in order to receive this exemption.[27] This is technically a liberalizing measure for the GSP, and effectively exempts the least-developed countries from negotiating pressures via the GSP. In reality, it will have little practical effect on the program. The thirty-two countries considered to be least developed are generally too small and uncompetitive to exceed the CNC in the first place. The only products from these countries that have exceeded the CNL in the past are jute products from Bangladesh and baseballs from Haiti.

The TTA also raises the *de minimis* level to a figure equal to $5 million in terms of the U.S. GNP in 1979; the amount is adjusted each year for changes in GNP. This amount was equal to $7.58 million in the 1984 product review. As can be seen from table 4–2, raising the *de minimis* level made a larger number of products eligible for continued GSP treatment. The 1984 review (effective 1985) was the first in which more than two countries were denied *de minimis* waivers.[28] It is conceivable that the raised *de minimis* figure could augment the negotiable aspects of the GSP program, although for the present the USTR continues its policy of denying waivers only when import-sensitivity may be alleged by a domestic industry.

Significance of the New Negotiability

This approach may appear incongruous with the principle of nonreciprocity in tariff preferences, but it is consistent with a long-standing U.S. view that GSP beneficiaries should assume greater obligations as their economies develop. In fact, the executive branch has always had discretion to curtail GSP benefits, both in domestic law and by international agreement. The United States insisted during the Tokyo Round discussions of the enabling clause that the GSP must be seen as a temporary program, and that the developing countries commit themselves to "fuller participation" in the liberal trade system.[29] The definition of *fuller participation* and the means for achieving it were never explicitly spelled out. Other GSP sponsors have introduced elements of reciprocity into their programs, but the negotiable eligibility established by the TTA is arguably the most radical interpretation of the enabling clause to date.

One of the harsher critics of this approach in the Congress is Representative Donald J. Pease (Dem.-Ohio), who described the new negotiability as "an instrument of economic blackmail." According to Pease, "This new emphasis on reciprocity not only increases the opportunities for abuse of the GSP, but actually violates the spirit, if not the letter of the [GATT].[30]

The new element of negotiable eligibility could prove to be an important tool for U.S. negotiators, particularly with countries that have large CNL exclusions. Even a comparatively small exclusion can be important if it represents a high percentage of a country's total or GSP-eligible exports to the United States. With nearly all of Zambia's GSP-eligible exports excluded by the CNL in 1985, U.S. negotiators theoretically have a large bargaining chip to use with that country. In reality the new negotiability of the GSP will be directed mostly at the top five GSP countries identified in table 4–3. The CNL exclusion in effect as of 1985 affects roughly half of the GSP-eligible products exported by these countries to the United States.

Countries might also be cajoled into making concessions to the United States when threatened by the lower (25 percent/$25 million) competitive-need limits. If applied across the board to all GSP-eligible products, these limits could cut GSP eligibility in half.

The leverage offered by the CNL should not be overstated, however. The beneficiary countries realize that the GSP renewal legislation does not address all of their complaints with the program, such as the exclusion of certain labor-intensive products. Because the president can only grant waivers for products that were eligible for the GSP in the first place, he cannot offer radically

Table 4-3
CNL Exclusions In Force, by Country, Following the 1984 GSP Review
(in $ thousands)[a]

Country	Dollar Value of Excluded Products	Excluded Products as a Percentage of	
		GSP-Eligible Products	Total Exports to United States
Taiwan	4,398,880	56.5	27.3
Mexico	3,137,414	59.5	17.2
Hong Kong	2,239,735	56.0	25.2
South Korea	1,139,742	38.1	10.1
Singapore	1,009,707	49.1	24.5
Brazil	602,009	31.9	7.3
Dominican Republic[b]	201,648	55.7	18.9
Chile	198,347	68.6	22.8
Argentina	158,510	47.3	15.2
Malaysia	145,941	33.1	5.2
Philippines	141,996	29.2	5.4
Colombia	106,964	52.7	8.5
Zambia	86,831	92.8	67.5
Peru	77,380	33.1	5.5
Venezuela	42,338	24.5	0.6
Haiti[b]	33,646	15.9	8.5
Turkey	13,661	41.5	2.9
India	7,824	2.5	0.2
Portugal	6,031	3.2	1.2
Total	$13,796,574	46.1	

Source: Calculated from information supplied by the Trade Representative GSP Information Center and from import statistics of the U.S. Department of Commerce.
[a] Figures are in terms of 1984 trade; exclusions are effective July 1, 1985.
[b]CBI country, for which GSP and competitive-need exclusions are irrelevant.

increased access to the U.S. market. Moreover, U.S. tariff rates are relatively low and dropping for most GSP products, which means that the margins of preference are not an attractive inducement for developing countries in many product categories.

The interest shown by the GSP beneficiary countries may be gauged by the requests they submitted in early 1985 for competitive-need waivers. Under the GSP regulations issued by the Office of the U.S. Trade Representative, waiver requests for the 1987 general review had to be submitted by May 31, 1985.[31] The great majority of the waiver requests were submitted by or on behalf of the governments of Mexico, Hong Kong, Taiwan, Singapore, and South Korea, and most were accepted by the USTR for review.[32] In contrast, Brazil did not submit any waiver requests at all. The Brazilian government reportedly felt that the general review is inconsistent with the principles of the GSP program, and refused to play along with the new game. Even though Brazil submitted no waiver requests, it may still benefit from the waivers. The USTR may grant waivers on some products for all advanced beneficiary countries, in order to avoid charges of discriminatory treatment.

Changes in Country and Product Eligibility

Country Eligibility

The Trade Act of 1974 enumerated several industrialized countries that the president is barred from designating as GSP beneficiary countries; all others are eligible for designation. Hungary was among these ineligible countries, but the TTA strikes Hungary from the list. The deletion does not automatically make Hungary eligible for the program. The country must first be designated by the president, who is bound by the designation eligibility criteria. As of this writing, Hungary has not been so designated.

Eligibility Criteria

The Trade Act of 1974, as amended in 1976 and 1979, spelled out several criteria that must be met by beneficiaries. Some of these criteria are mandatory, and others may be waived by the president for reasons of national economic interest.

The president cannot designate any country that:

1. is communist, unless that country is a member of the GATT and the IMF, and is not dominated by international communism;
2. is a member of the Organization of Petroleum Exporting Countries, or any other arrangement to withhold vital commodities from international trade;[33] or
3. affords preferential treatment to the products of a developed country that has significant adverse effects on the United States.

The president must also deny GSP eligibility for countries that engage in the following practices, but may waive these considerations for reasons of national economic interest:

1. if the country has nationalized, expropriated, or otherwise seized ownership or control of property owned by a U.S. citizen or corporation, unless the president determined that prompt, adequate, and effective compensation has been or is being made, or good faith negotiations are underway;
2. if the country does not cooperate with the United States to prevent production and traffic in narcotic drugs and other controlled substances;

3. if the country fails to recognize as binding or does not enforce arbitral awards in favor of U.S. citizens or corporations; and

4. if the country aids or abets international terrorism.

Beyond these criteria, the 1974 act lists considerations that the president "shall take into account" in designating beneficiaries, including the country's desire to be designated, its level of economic development, whether or not the other major developed countries are extending GSP treatment to the country, and the extent to which the country has assured the United States that it will provide equitable and reasonable access to its markets and basic commodity resources.

These designation criteria have not proven to be a difficult barrier to eligibility; nearly all developing countries have been designated as GSP beneficiaries. As of 1984, there were 114 independent countries, twenty-six non-independent countries and territories, and three associations of countries (the Caribbean Community, the Andean Group, and ASEAN) that were designated for the program. The only countries that have lost GSP eligibility due to violations of the criteria are Afghanistan and Ethiopia. Of the countries that are not specifically ineligible for designation because of their level of economic development, the only ones that do not receive GSP treatment are Ethiopia, most OPEC members, and most third–world communist countries.[34]

The New Criteria

The renewal legislation makes no additions to the list of mandatory criteria that may not be waived, but does add to the other considerations that the president must weigh. These new criteria will form part of the U.S. negotiating objectives in the neoreciprocity described earlier in this chapter.

Workers Rights. U.S. labor groups and human rights advocates urged that the Congress make GSP benefits conditional upon a country's respect for human and union rights. This request stemmed from two concerns. First, the groups were concerned that by exploiting workers and denying them the right to organize and bargain collectively, producers in the developing countries prevent the benefits of the GSP program from being shared equitably. Second, U.S. labor unions view the denial of workers rights abroad as an indirect subsidy on exports. By keeping wages and benefits down to extremely low levels, foreign producers can enjoy a substantial competitive advantage over their rivals in the United States. Not coincidentally, the countries that are most often singled out for criticism in the area of workers rights are among the very same countries that U.S. labor unions consider most threatening.

In considering whether to designate a country for the GSP, or continue its status as a beneficiary, the president must now determine (based on annual reports to the Congress) "if such country has not taken or is not taking steps to

afford internationally recognized workers rights to workers in the country."
These "internationally recognized workers rights" are defined in the legislation
to include:

1. The right of association
2. The right to organize and bargain collectively
3. A prohibition on the use of any form of forced or compulsory labor
4. A minimum age for the employment of children
5. Acceptable conditions of work with respect to minimum wages, hours of
   work, and occupational safety and health.

The criteria enumerated in the legislation are still somewhat vague. It is
uncertain, for example, whether the right to strike is internationally recognized,
or if membership in the International Labor Organization is a necessary or
sufficient condition for respecting labor rights.

Intellectual Property Rights. As discussed in chapter 2, U.S. industries that
rely on the sanctity of patents, trademarks, copyrights, and authors' rights have
pressed the U.S. government to enforce their rights in trade negotiations. The
Trade Act of 1974 required that the president consider whether a potential GSP
beneficiary country had nationalized, expropriated, or otherwise seized control
of property owned by U.S. citizens. The TTA amends this criterion to clarify
that it covers protection for patents, trademarks, and copyrights. This protection only seems to extend, however, to cases where the government in question
is the violator. It appears to have little bearing in cases involving violations by
private firms or individuals. The TTA also requires that the president "take into
account":

> the extent to which such country is providing adequate and effective means
> under its laws for foreign nationals to secure, to exercise, and to enforce
> exclusive rights in intellectual property, including patents, trademarks, and
> copyrights.

Copper Exports. The act requires that the president take into account "the
extent to which such country has assured the United States that it will refrain
from engaging in unreasonable export practices." The act offers no definition or
enumeration of "unreasonable" practices, but the legislative history of the
amendment indicates that it arose from the frustration felt by some members of
Congress over President Reagan's refusal in 1984 to grant relief to the domestic
copper industry under the escape clause. The author of the amendment, Sen.
Max Baucus (Dem.-Montana), stated in a colloquy on the floor of the Senate
that "unreasonable export practices" include the export of copper in volumes
and at prices which cause injury to the domestic U.S. copper industry.[35] It is
unlikely that this concern will lead the administration to apply this provision

against copper exporters. President Reagan rejected a USITC recommendation to provide import relief to the U.S. copper industry in 1984, and is under no obligation to use this new language to deny GSP benefits to copper exporters.

Investment Practices and Trade in Services. The TTA endorses the Reagan administration's new issues (see chapter 2) by requiring that the president take into account "the extent to which such country has taken action to:

1. reduce distorting investment practices and policies (including export performance requirements)
2. reduce or eliminate barriers to trade in services.

Significance of the New Criteria

The renewal act calls for the president to submit a report to the Congress by January 4, 1988 on the application of the new designation criteria. This report will emphasize the application of the new considerations.

The chief effect of these criteria is to create a new set of U.S. negotiating objectives with the GSP beneficiary countries. During hearings on beneficiary country practices held in July 1985, U.S. businesses, trade organizations, and interest groups charged many of the BDCs with unfair or illegal trade practices, such as excessive restrictions on access to the country's home market, failure to protect workers rights, and violations of intellectual property rights. At least some of these charges will be accepted by U.S. trade negotiators as objectives in their discussions with GSP beneficiary countries.

The country practices that were criticized in these hearings have implications beyond the "new negotiability" of the GSP. The hearings gave domestic U.S. interests an opportunity to air their complaints in a formal setting, and it is quite possible that the hearings will provide raw material for the *National Trade Estimate* that the USTR must now prepare annually (see chapter 2). In brief, the complaints may be the subject of negotiations that extend well past consideration of a country's GSP eligibility.

Limit on Per Capita GNP

The Congress decided against graduating any countries by name, but did establish an unprecedented limit on the development level for beneficiary countries. Any nation that achieves a per capita GNP of $8,500 or more (as reported by the World Bank) will be graduated from the program after two years. This ceiling figure will be increased annually to reflect growth in the nominal GNP of the United States, but the figure will only grow at one-half the rate of growth in U.S. GNP. During a country's final two years of eligibility, all of its products will be subject to the lower competitive-need limit.

The $8,500 limit will not affect many beneficiary countries. Bahrein, Bermuda, Brunei, and Nauru appear to have already reached this mark, and Singapore's current income of about $6,700 per capita could grow beyond the limit by the early 1990s. No other countries are likely to be affected in the near future, particularly because the wealthier OPEC members are already excluded from eligibility.

Product Eligibility

As discussed already, the president designates individual products for eligibility, based on advice received from the USTR. The USTR has deemed several products to be import-sensitive in the context of GSP, and therefore ineligible for the program. Among the items that the USTR has determined to be import-sensitive are footwear, most handbags, luggage, flat goods, work gloves, and leather wearing apparel. The TTA adds these enumerated products to the list of those that are permanently excluded from eligibility. The new language makes the exclusions permanent by statute, and ensures that the USTR cannot reverse its judgment and designate the products for the GSP.

Administrative Changes in the Program

Duration of the GSP. The original GSP authorization expired on January 3, 1985. The GSP renewal act came into effect on January 4, 1985, and will last until July 4, 1993. This eight-and-one-half-year extension was a compromise between the ten-year extension passed by the Senate and the five years which the House approved. An extra year was added by the congressional conferees so that the next GSP renewal bill can be considered after the 1992 presidential election is over.

Date for the Implementation of Annual Changes. Prior to the TTA, changes in GSP eligibility made during the annual reviews were implemented on March 31 of the following year. The TTA rolls the implementation date forward to July 1 of the following year. This step was taken in response to requests from BDC exporters and U.S. importers, who wished to have greater lead time following to adjust to the outcome of the reviews.

Changes in the Review Process. Changes were made in the annual review procedure through informal commitment. In the course of the renewal process, certain domestic agricultural interests expressed their dissatisfaction with the existing practices. They argued that the reconsideration of petitions that were already turned down in previous annual reviews is burdensome and time-consuming. Given the strength of these interests in the Congress, the administration decided to placate them by clarifying and modifying its policies. U.S. Trade Representative Brock described certain procedures to be followed in administering the renewed GSP program, including a three-year waiting period for GSP designations following an unsuccessful petition that underwent a full review, an expanded opportunity for interested parties to comment on petitions before a final decision is made, and public hearings in the GSP general review.

Customs Service Consultations with the USTR. The TTA directs the U.S. Customs Service to consult with the USTR when it prepares regulations concerning the GSP. This is a technical amendment, although it seems likely that the USTR will use this consultative power to ensure that the Customs Service regulations do not impose unnecessary burdens on the GSP beneficiary nations.

Agricultural Exports

Bread for the World (BFW) expressed its concern to the Congress that the export orientation of the GSP might contribute to the diversion of foodstuffs from the domestic markets of beneficiary countries. In response to these concerns, the Congress added the following requirement to the GSP:

> The appropriate agencies of the United States shall assist beneficiary developing countries to develop and implement measures designed to assure that the agricultural sectors of their economies are not directed to export markets to the detriment of the production of foodstuffs for their citizenry.

The intent of this provision is similar to that of a BFW-sponsored proviso in the Caribbean Basin Economic Recovery Act, which requires that CBI beneficiary countries prepare a Stable Food Production plan before they can export meat and dairy products duty-free to the United States. This plan must ensure that basic foodstuffs will not be diverted from domestic consumption. There are two important differences, however, between the requirements in the CBI and the new GSP legislation. The CBI's Stable Food Production Plan is mandatory, and the burden is placed on the governments of the beneficiary countries. The additional requirement will not endanger any nation's eligibility for GSP benefits, while the burden (if any) is placed on the agencies of the U.S. Government.

Notes

1. For an interesting discussion of the development of the "special and more favorable" treatment principle, see Abdulqawi A. Yusuf, "'Differential and More Favourable Treatment': The GATT Enabling Clause," *Journal of World Trade Law* 14, no. 6

(Nov.–Dec. 1980). See also chapter 25 of John H. Jackson, *World Trade and the Law of GATT* (Charlottesville, Virginia: The Michie Company, 1969).

2. Yusuf, *op. cit.*

3. See the testimony of Dr. Alfred Eckes, chairman of the U.S. International Trade Commission, in United States Senate, Committee on Finance, Subcommittee on International Trade, *Proposed Renewal of the Generalized System of Preferences—1984.* 98th Congress, 2d session, Senate Hearing 98–697 (January 27, 1984), p. 15. (The volume is cited hereinafter as *Senate GSP Hearings.*)

4. This is not to say that tariff liberalization is against the interests of developing countries. A quantitative study of a hypothetical, across-the-board tariff cut of 50 percent in the Tokyo Round negotiations concluded that "the developing countries stand more to gain from MFN tariff cuts than they will lose from the simultaneous erosion of their GSP preferential tariff margins." The calculated benefits exceeded the costs by about four to one. See R.E. Baldwin and T. Murray, "MFN Tariff Reductions and Developing Country Trade Benefits Under the GSP," *The Economic Journal,* 87 no. 345 (March 1977), p. 44.

5. See Bela Balassa and Carol Balassa, "Industrial Protection in the Developed Countries," *The World Economy* 7, no. 2 (June 1984), table 2.

6. A product's eligibility for GSP treatment is noted in the tariff schedules by the letter A in the far left column. An asterisk next to the A indicates that one or more countries are excluded from GSP benefits for that product.

7. The USTR has deemed the following products to be import-sensitive in the context of GSP, and therefore ineligible for the program: (1) luggage, flat goods, work gloves, leather wearing apparel, and most handbags, (2) canned tuna fish, (3) petroleum and petroleum products, (4) certain processed agricultural goods, (5) rum, and (6) tobacco.

8. It might also be argued that excluding these products has little ultimate effect on the competitive position of the beneficiary countries, given the fact that U.S. imports of most of these products are already dominated by the developing nations. By the same token, if only some of the beneficiary countries were eligible for GSP treatment for these products, then the program could impart a competitive benefit to the less advanced LDCs.

9. U.S. International Trade Commission, *Operation of the Trade Agreements Program,* 36th Annual Report. USITC Publication 1725 (July 1985), p. 219.

10. *Ibid.*

11. Eckes, *op. cit.*, p. 7. The figures do not reflect which of these products are actually dutiable for countries that do not receive GSP treatment.

12. Ambassador Brock's statement was made at a luncheon session hosted by the Overseas Development Council in September 1984. It was published as "U.S. Trade Policy Toward Developing Countries" in Ernest H. Preeg, ed., *Hard Bargaining Ahead: U.S. Trade Policy and Developing Countries,* U.S.–Third World Policy Perspectives no. 4 (Washington, D.C.: Overseas Development Council, 1985), p. 37.

13. U.S. International Trade Commission, *Changes in Import Trends Resulting from Excluding Selected Imports from the Generalized System of Preferences.* USITC Publication 1384 (May 1983), p. iii.

14. For purposes of GSP reviews, *product* means a five-digit item in the Tariff Schedules of the United States.

15. There is no internationally accepted definition for the NICs, nor any standard list. The TTA does, however, define a category of countries that will receive tighter scrutiny in the GSP general review. See note 26, below.

16. It is important to distinguish between the modest proposals advanced by third-world statesmen such as Raul Prebisch, and the overblown expectations that these proposals raised in some quarters. For a discussion of the preferences debate during the 1960s, see Sidney Weintraub, *Trade Preferences for Less-Developed Countries: An Analysis of United States Trade Policy* (New York: Praeger, 1966).

17. For examples of the recommendations, see Organization of American States, Inter-American Economic and Social Council, *Report of the Technical Meeting on the United States Generalized System of Preferences* (Washington, D.C.: June 1983); Stuart Tucker, "The U.S. GSP Program: Trade Preferences and Development," *Policy Focus* 6 (Overseas Development Council, September 1984); and the testimony of the Office of the Secretary General, United Nations Conference on Trade and Development, in *Senate GSP Hearings*, pp. 328–47.

18. See the testimony of Michael A. Samuels of the U.S. Chamber of Commerce in *Senate GSP Hearings, op. cit.*, especially p. 124; and W. Henry Parsons, GSP Subcommittee Chairman of the American Association of Exporters and Importers, *ibid.*, especially pp. 58–59.

19. Testimony of Clayton Yeutter, in U.S. House of Representatives, Committee on Ways and Means, *Possible Renewal of the Generalized System of Preferences—Part i*, Serial 98–46, 98th Congress, 1st Session (Washington, D.C.: U.S. Government Printing Office, 1984), p. 38.

20. See Chapter 2.

21. See the testimony of Stephen Koplan of the AFL–CIO in *Senate GSP Hearings, op. cit.*, pp. 87–99; and the statement of Bread for the World, *ibid.*, pp. 290–99.

22. Koplan, *op. cit.*, p. 94.

23. See *Senate GSP Hearings, op. cit.*, especially the testimony and statements of the Leather Products Coalition, the American Iron and Steel Institute, the Bicycle Manufacturers Association of America, and the American pipe Fittings Association.

24. The executive branch has always had the ability to limit the GSP benefits of the BDCs. The 1984 amendments make this authority more explicit and constitute direct congressional approval of the Reagan administration's intentions.

25. The value of a waiver is calculated not by the total imports from a BDC of the product in question, but by the marginal value of the imports that exceed the CNL.

26. The twin criteria are a per capita GNP of $5,000 or more or duty-free GSP imports into the United States accounting for 10 percent or more of total U.S. imports under the program. Based on 1984 data, these criteria would point to Bahrein, Bermuda, Brunei, Hong Kong, Israel, South Korea, Nauru, Singapore, Taiwan, and Trinidad and Tobago. Four of these countries (Bahrein, Bermuda, Brunei, and Nauru) are scheduled for GSP graduation due to high per capita GNPs in excess of $8,500; Trinidad and Tobago is a beneficiary country of the Caribbean Basin Initiative; and Israel benefits from the U.S.–Israeli free trade area.

27. On April 29, 1985, President Reagan designated the following thirty-two countries as least developed:

Bangladesh	Lesotho
Benin	Malawi
Bhutan	Maldives
Botswana	Mali
Burkina Faso	Nepal
Burundi	Niger
Cape Verde	Rwanda
Central African Republic	Sao Tome and Principe
Chad	Sierra Leone
Comoros	Somalia
Djibouti	Sudan
Equatorial Guinea	Tanzania
Gambia	Togo
Guinea	Uganda
Guinea–Bissau	Western Samoa
Haiti	Yemen Arab Republic (Sanaa)

28. The following countries were denied *de minimis* waivers in the 1984 review: Argentina, Brazil, Hong Kong, Israel, Mexico, South Korea, and Taiwan.

29. Yusuf, *op. cit.*

30. Donald J. Pease and J. William Gould, "The New GSP: Fair Trade with the Third World?" *World Policy Journal* 2, no. 2 (Spring 1985): 360.

31. *Federal Register* 50, no. 31 (February 14, 1985): 6294–97.

32. The USTR accepted virtually all petitions for review, provided that the product was eligible for the GSP, would still be dutiable following full implementation of the Tokyo Round tariff reductions in 1987, and did not appear to be import-sensitive on the basis of prima facie evidence (for example, an outstanding countervailing duty order, or a recently rejected petition for designation or redesignation).

33. An exception to this rule was made for Venezuela, Ecuador, and Indonesia.

34. The People's Republic of China is not a GSP beneficiary, due in part to the fact that it is not a GATT member. Countries that are "dominated by international communism" (which is interpreted to mean Soviet-bloc) include Bulgaria, Cuba, Laos, North Korea, and Vietnam. Albania is not considered to be a Soviet-bloc nation, but has not been designated for the GSP because it is not a GATT or IMF member, either.

35. *Congressional Record*, 98th Congress, 2nd session (September 19, 1984), pp. S11492–93.

Part II
Trade-Remedy Laws

5
The Escape Clause

The escape clause (section 201 of the Trade Act of 1974) provides U.S. industries that suffer serious injury from import competition a means of seeking temporary relief. No other trade-remedy law offers such sweeping relief—restrictions on imports from all foreign sources—but it also imposes the highest standards of proof from the petitioner. The TTA amends section 201 in two ways: the indicators of "serious injury" are further defined, and the procedures for congressional overrides of presidential decisions are altered.

The Escape Clause and the GATT

The term *escape clause* refers both to article XIX of the GATT, and the U.S. domestic legislation under which article XIX may be invoked. The escape clause is a sort of safety valve in the machinery of the GATT that allows countries to temporarily escape from the obligations they have made to their trading partners under the agreement. It was inserted in the GATT at the insistence of the United States because of congressional concern that trade liberalization might have unforeseen and adverse consequences for some industries. The article states that:

> If, as a result of unforeseen developments and of the effect of [trade concessions] . . . any product is being imported into the territory of [a] contracting party in such increased quantities and under such conditions as to cause or threaten serious injury to domestic producers. . . the contracting party shall be free . . . to suspend the obligation in whole or in part or to withdraw or modify the concession.

The article and its implementing statutes are not intended to establish permanent protection, but rather to allow for orderly adjustment by domestic industries.[1] During the period of temporary relief, the industry is expected to set its house in order and prepare for renewed global competition.

Article XIX stipulates that any use of the escape clause requires prior notice to other contracting parties, followed by consultations, but in actual practice "critical circumstances" usually delay consultations until after the action has already been taken. The affected trading partners then have the right to retaliate by withdrawing "substantially equivalent concessions" affecting the goods of the party invoking the escape clause. In lieu of retaliation, agreements may be negotiated in which the trade-restricting country pays "compensation" to the other nations by lowering barriers on products or interest to the affected countries.

The escape clause serves a useful purpose in the GATT system. It simultaneously allows member countries to impose trade restrictions if imports become disruptive, while still requiring nations to be mindful of their obligations to their trading partners. In this way, the system can bend without breaking. If there were no such safeguard built into the trade regime, departures from trade obligations negotiated in the GATT could lead to a general unraveling of these commitments. However, the escape clause continues to be a consistent source of tension within the GATT. Several issues divide the member states, including the precise standard for determining injury to a domestic industry, the failure of many countries taking escape-clause actions to notify their trading partners in advance, and the growing practice of some countries (including the United States) to apply import restrictions selectively to the principal suppliers, rather than in a nondiscriminatory fashion, in a manner that allows them to evade the GATT requirements for compensation. A special committee of the GATT has been attempting to resolve these issues by drafting a safeguards code, but progress thus far has been slow.[2]

Section 201

In the United States, article XIX of the GATT is implemented at the national level by section 201 of the Trade Act of 1974.[3] Unlike the antisubsidy and antidumping laws (see chapter 6), the escape clause does not involve concurrent investigations by both the U.S. International Trade Commission (USITC) and the Department of Commerce. The USITC has sole jurisdiction over proceedings under section 201, up until the time that it reports to the president. If and when the USITC recommends that import relief be granted, however, all federal agencies involved in economic policy (and several that are not) take part in advising the White House.

Investigations begin under section 201 when a group that is representative of an industry (for example, a trade association, firm, union, or combination of the above) submits a petition to the USITC. Proceedings may also be started by the USITC on its own motion, or upon the request of the president, the USTR, the House Ways and Means Committee, or the Senate Finance Committee. Nearly all investigations are initiated by domestic industries.[4]

The petition is required to lay out a *prima facie* case for import relief, meaning that it must present information showing that increasing imports cause or threaten to cause serious injury to the domestic industry. The petition must precisely describe the product and its tariff classification, state the levels of domestic production and imports, and explain how these imports cause or threaten serious injury to the domestic industry. The commission further requires that the petition state the purpose of filing for such relief and describe the efforts undertaken by firms and workers to compete more effectively with foreign producers. Petitioners are not required to show that foreign imports are unfairly traded, although such allegations can be included at the petitioner's discretion.

After the USITC accepts the petition, it has six months to reach a final decision. The commission directs its economic and legal staffs to commence an investigation into the allegations made by the petitioners. The staff collects information from the affected domestic industry, government agencies, domestic importers, foreign producers, trade associations, and other interested parties through mailed questionnaires and on-site interviews. The data forms the basis of a prehearing staff report submitted to the commissioners. Petitioners, respondents, and other interested parties submit prehearing briefs to the commission.

About three to four months after the submission of a petition, the USITC holds a public hearing. All interested parties are given an opportunity to present their cases to the commission, and to challenge any views presented by other parties. Following the hearing, the USITC staff prepares a report for the commissioners presenting the facts of the case, together with the possible options for remedy. When the commission reconvenes in a public meeting, it votes on whether or not the criteria for relief are met. (These criteria are discussed shortly.) If the majority of the commission votes negatively, then the case is immediately terminated. If the USITC finds injury, then another vote is held on the appropriate form of remedy. A tie vote is considered to be an affirmative decision.

The remedy vote is taken separately, and usually at a later date. In the interim, the commissioners consult with one another over the remedies available. The commission attempts to reach a majority recommendation, which (not unlike Supreme Court decisions) often requires considerable debate and compromise. Congress urges the commission to reach majority decisions since if it does not, Congress cannot override the president's decision.

After the USITC has voted on the question of injury and an appropriate form of remedy, it transmits a report to the president. The report must be made no later than six months after the petition was filed. The White House then has sixty days to decide whether to accept, reject, or modify the commission's recommendations. If the president does decide to offer relief, then it must go into effect within fifteen days. The only exception is when the president decides in favor of orderly marketing agreements, then the White House has ninety days to negotiate them with the supplying countries and implement them.

Section 201 establishes a presumption of approval by stating that the president *shall* provide relief, unless the chief executive determines that this would not be in the national economic interest. In actual practice, the White House has found that import relief is not in the national economic interest more often than it has granted relief. The president does not make the decision independently, but is assisted by the bureaucracy through the interagency review process. Starting at the working-level Trade Policy Staff Committee (TPSC) and percolating up through the Trade Policy Review Group (TPRG), the committees give over a dozen separate departments and agencies an opportunity to air their views.[5] Prior to an administrative reorganization in early 1985, the final recommendation to the president would come from the cabinet-level Trade Policy Committee (TPC) chaired by the U.S. Trade Representative. Early in the second term of the Reagan administration, a new Economic Policy Council (EPC) was established, with the secretary of the treasury as chairperson.

Agencies particularly concerned with trade policy implications include the Office of the U.S. Trade Representative and the Departments of Agriculture, Commerce and Labor, but they are not the only participants. Agencies concerned with strategic and political foreign policy concerns, such as the State and Defense Departments, are likely to oppose strong measures that could lead to complications overseas. The Council of Economic Advisors and the Treasury frequently oppose granting relief, given their global economic perspectives. These aspects of section 201 cases are obviously more pronounced when the product is of major importance (for example, steel) than they are for less important goods (such as asparagus).

Whatever the president decides to do, he must report his decision promptly to the Congress. If the White House decides to offer relief that differs from the USITC's recommendations, or to provide no relief whatsoever to the domestic industry, the Congress may override this decision. This has not yet occurred.

If the United States does invoke the escape clause, its trading partners are entitled to compensation throughout the period of relief. Failure to provide adequate compensation gives other countries a right to retaliate. Section 123 of the Trade Act of 1974 provides the president with the negotiating authority to reach such agreements. The section states that the president:

> may enter into trade agreements with foreign countries or instrumentalities for the purpose of granting new concessions as compensation in order to maintain the general level of reciprocal and mutually advantageous concessions; and may

proclaim such modification or continuance of any existing duty, or such continuance of duty-free or excise treatment, as he determines to be required or appropriate to carry out any such agreement.

Agreements made under the section 123 negotiating authority must be limited in both degree and duration. The president cannot reduce any duty rate by more than 30 percent of its existing rate, and the tariff concession must be phased out along with the escape-clause restrictions. To date, the section 123 authority has been used to negotiate compensation only two times since the enactment of the Trade Act of 1974.

Relief actions are subject to review and modfication. The president may reduce or terminate relief any time that he considers this to be in the national interest, after receiving a report from the USITC on the probable economic effects of the extension, reduction, or termination of import relief. Section 203 of the Trade Act of 1974 requires the USITC to monitor developments in the industry that receives relief, including the efforts taken in adjusting to import competition.

Six to nine months before the import relief program is due to expire, the industry may petition the commission for an extension of relief. After holding a hearing on the matter, the USITC will advise the president on whether an extension is warranted. Relief can be extended for no more than three additional years, and at levels no higher than those in the last year of the initial relief plan.

The Standards for Providing Relief

Unlike the trade-remedy laws relating to dumping and subsidization (see chapter 6), the escape clause does not specifically deal with unfairly traded imports. The principal concern in this statute is the welfare of domestic industries, rather than the trade practices of their foreign competitors.

The USITC's investigation centers on whether or not the domestic industry faces "serious injury" or the threat of serious injury. This is a more demanding standard than the "material injury" test in antidumping duty (AD) and counter-vailing duty (CVD) cases. The Trade Act of 1974 does not explicitly define serious injury, but sets out criteria that the commissioners must apply in reaching a determination. In order to find serious injury, the commission must find:

the significant idling of productive facilities in the industry, the inability of a significant number of firms to operate at a reasonable level of profit, and a significant unemployment or underemployment within the industry.

The word *and* in this passage has been the source of serious dispute between the commission and some members of Congress. Some commissioners interpret *and* to mean that all three criteria must be met in order for it to find serious injury, but congressional critics argue that no one factor should be considered dispositive of injury. In a 1984 case involving nonrubber footwear, the commissioners unanimously found that the domestic industry did not suffer serious injury. Their decision was based on stable production and employment in the industry, and reasonable profits (particularly for the larger producers).[6] The commissioners also noted that the domestic producers were themselves major importers of shoes, accounting for about one-third to one-half of all imports. The profits from these captive imports (items imported by domestic producers) contributed to the overall level of profitability in the industry, but were not found to be the sole source of profit. The USITC's decision was erroneously interpreted by some critics to mean that the single issue of profits led to the negative finding. The uproar over the commission's negative decision led to an effort to change the definition of serious injury in section 201.

In order to find that an industry faces a threat of serious injury, the USITC looks for:

a decline in sales, a higher and growing inventory, and a downward trend in production, profits, and wages, or employment (or increasing underemployment) in the domestic industry concerned.

If the commission determines that the industry faces serious injury or the threat of serious injury, its next step is to establish causation (that is, to determine whether increasing imports are a substantial cause of serious injury or the threat thereof). The legislation defines *substantial cause* to mean "a cause which is important and not less than any other cause." Some observers believe that the U.S. law imposes a stricter standard in this instance than does the GATT, which requires that the imports be an "important cause" of injury. *Important* is a less demanding term than *substantial,* in that a cause may be "important" without being "not less than any other cause."

The commission restricts its inquiry to narrowly defined economic considerations; the president is required by the law to take a broader view of the national economic interest in these decisions. In addition to receiving the recommendations of the USITC, section 203 requires that the president consider "the probable effectiveness of import relief as a means to promote adjustment, [and] the efforts being made or to be implemented by the inudstry concerned to adjust to import competition." Section 203 further directs the president to take into account several considerations that tend to militate against deciding in favor of relief, including the effect relief would have on consumers; the impact on price, availability, and competition in the domestic market; the effect of import relief on the international economic interests of the United States; and the impact that any foreign retaliation would have on U.S. industries and firms. Other considerations might tend to favor relief, such as the concentration of imports in the United States, and the economic and social costs to taxpayers, communities, and workers if relief is not provided.

Available Remedies

If the commission reaches an affirmative or split decision, it must determine level and type of import relief that would be necessary to prevent or remedy the injury.[7] This relief may take the form of duties or other import restrictions. As an alternative to import relief, the commission may recommend that trade adjustment assistance be offered to the workers and firms that suffer from import competition. Adjustment assistance is basically an extended form of unemployment compensation that is intended to ease the transition to other types of employment.[8] It is not technically considered to be a form of import relief.

The commission may recommend import restrictions that take the form of higher duties (which cannot increase by more than 50 percentage points *ad valorem* above the existing rate), tariff-rate quotas, quantitative restrictions (quotas), or any combination of these measures.[9] If the commissioners find that the injury is caused or contributed to by the tariff benefits provided by the Generalized System of Preferences (see chapter 4), free trade arrangements such as those with Israel (see chapter 3) and the Caribbean Basin, or the TSUS 806.30/807 program, then they may recommend the suspension of special tariff treatment for the product.[10] These suspensions can be all or part of the relief. However, any time relief is granted, the product is suspended from the GSP. The plan must be of defined duration and cannot exceed five years. In cases where the recommended relief is for three or more years, the law requires that, to the extent feasible, relief should be phased down in its final years. The first reduction in the level of relief should take place no later than the third year.

The president may accept or reject the USITC recommendation to provide import relief and/or adjustment assistance. If he does provide relief, he is not bound by the plan presented by the USITC. The White House can provide any of the import relief options that were available to the commission, and may also choose to negotiate orderly marketing agreements (OMAs) with the principal suppliers of the products in question. An OMA Is a formal agreement between an exporting and an importing country, in which they jointly agree to limit shipments to a certain level. As a formal remedy under the escape clause, an OMA may be enforced at the border of the importing country. This alternative is a grey-area measure that is outside the strict letter of GATT article XIX. In the

GATT system, escape-clause relief is intended to be applied in a nondiscriminatory fashion, meaning that it should apply equally to all trading partners, and paid for with compensation to one's trading partners. Orderly marketing agreements are often criticized for being inconsistent with this principle.

Past Experience in Escape-Clause Cases

The domestic industries seeking protection from import competition have been rewarded import relief on relatively few occasions. Between the implementation of the Trade Act of 1974 and the end of 1985, the USITC completed 55 escape-clause investigations. The commission found injury or the threat of injury on 32 occasions (58.2 percent of the time). Of the possible forms of relief, the commission has shown a slight predeliction for tariffs, which it has recommended 14 times. Eleven investigations resulted in the recommendation of quotas. In three cases, the USITC recommended that trade adjustment assistance be extended in lieu of import relief. Tariff-rate quotas were recommended in two cases, while in the remaining two investigations the commissioners could not agree on a majority recommendation.

U.S. presidents have received 32 USITC recommendations that import relief and/or adjustment assistance be provided for U.S. firms and workers. The White House has provided no relief at all in 13 (40.2 percent) of these 32 cases, adjustment assistance in 6 cases (18.8 percent), and import relief (with or without adjustment assistance) in another 13 cases (40.2 percent). In all, U.S. petitioners have been rewarded with import relief and/or adjustment assistance in 19 out of 55 cases (34.5 percent).

Presidents Ford, Carter, and Reagan have shown different patterns in their decisions. President Ford held a definite preference for adjustment assistance, which he extended in 5 of the 9 cases that he decided. He provided relief in only one instance, and extended no relief at all in 3 cases. By contrast, President Carter never offered adjustment assistance to firms or workers in an escape-clause case, and opted for import relief in 8 of the 17 cases that came to his desk. President Reagan provided import relief 3 times, denied relief once, and extended adjustment assistance once. (President Reagan's decision to negotiate voluntary restraint agreements with foreign steel suppliers does not technically constitute granting import relief under the escape clause, but we count it here as an affirmative decision; see chapter 7).

The relatively low success rate has probably discouraged escape-clause petitions; the number filed dropped dramatically after 1977. Petitioners are more likely to seek relief under other statutes, which impose less demanding injury standards and are subject to less presidential discretion.

Another notable aspect of past escape-clause considerations is the executive's refusal to implement the USITC's recommended remedy. Of the thirty-two plans submitted by the commission to the White House, not a single one has ever been accepted in exactly the same form. Presidents have provided relief that resembled the majority's recommendation in just eight cases.

How the TTA Changes the Escape Clause

Criteria for Serious Injury

The USITC's refusal to recommend import relief in the 1984 nonrubber footwear case caused an uproar in the Congress, which set about amending the serious-injury criteria in section 201. The impact of these changes may not be as far-reaching as their sponsors had hoped. The most important of these amendments states that:

> The presence or absence of any factor which the Commission is required to evaluate . . . shall not necessarily be dispositive of whether an article is being imported into the United States in such increased quantities as to be a substantial cause of serious injury to the domestic injury.

The congressional intent of this amendment is to obviate future negative decisions based on the absence of any one indicator of serious injury. The authors of the amendment apparently believed that the commission's 1984 footwear decision was based on an inordinate attention to the issue of profitability in the shoe industry. A careful reading of the USITC report, however, reveals that the commissioners not only considered the issue of profits, but also based their decision on production and employment data.[11] Even if the commission had been instructed in 1984 that no one factor should be dispositive, it would not have reached a different decision.

The TTA states that "the term 'significant idling of productive facilities' includes the closing of plants or the underutilization of productive capacity." In the criterion that "growing inventory(ies) are indicative of the threat of serious injury," the inventories are defined by the TTA to include those "maintained by domestic producers, importers, wholesalers or retailers." In each case, the new language merely codifies the commission's existing interpretation of the law.

The House and Senate conferees stated in their conference report that "the Commission should, wherever possible, exclude profits derived from captive imports from the operations of the domestic industry." The authors of the conference report were concerned that the commission had placed too great an emphasis on the import practices of domestic footwear producers in the 1984 case, but in fact the USITC reached its conclusions regarding profitability solely on the basis of profits from domestic operations.

The USITC reconsidered the nonrubber footwear petition in 1985, and completely reversed its unanimous finding of no serious injury. On the basis of this 180-degree turnaround, it might be concluded that the 1984 amendments to the serious-injury criteria have effected a major change. A closer examination reveals that this is not the case. The commissioners stressed in their 1985 report on nonrubber footwear that their new findings were based entirely on changed circumstances and new information.[12] This is not to say, however, that the 1984 amendments will not affect future cases. It is possible that positive determinations in some instances will hinge on the treatment of individual factors that might otherwise have been dispositive of injury.

Joint Resolutions to Override Presidential Decisions

The TTA amends section 201 to allow the Congress to use joint resolutions to override presidential decisions in escape-clause cases. This amendment partially restores a right that the Congress had enjoyed since 1974 but appeared to have lost in 1983. The Trade Act of 1974 had given the Congress the power to use concurrent resolutions to put in place the import relief recommended by the USITC in cases arising under the escape clause, even if the president refused to grant relief. Concurrent resolutions require passage in both houses, but do not require the president's signature and do not have the force of law. In other words, the Congress could contravene the president with a simple majority vote, with no opportunity for the president to exercise a veto. This authority was never actually used by the Congress, although the threat of its use may have influenced some presidential decisions.[13]

The constitutionality of this provision, together with some 200 other legislative vetoes, was put into serious question by a 1983 Supreme Court decision that concerned immigration law rather than trade policy (*Chadha* v. *Immigration and Naturalization Service*). The Court found that it is unconstitutional for a single chamber of the Congress to use resolutions as legislative vetoes on executive decisions, as this violates the principle of checks and balances between the executive and legislative branches of government. The Court's decision put in doubt the validity of the congressional power to override the president in escape-clause cases.

The TTA amendment is designed to preserve the heretofore unused congressional prerogative by substituting joint resolutions for concurrent resolutions. Joint resolutions have the force of law and may be vetoed by the president. By the same token, the Congress can override the president's veto when both houses can muster a two-thirds majority. The principal difference between concurrent and joint resolutions is that the latter would ultimately require a two-thirds majority in order to override the president, whereas the former requires a simple majority vote. Because the congressional veto in section 201 cases has never been exercised, nor has its constitutionality been challenged, it cannot be stated with absolute certainty that the issue has been entirely resolved by the TTA language.

Notes

1. For an interesting discussion of the theory and practice of adjustment under the protection of the escape clause, see U.S. International Trade Commission, *The Effectiveness of Escape Clause Relief in Promoting Adjustment to Import Competition.* USITC Publication 1229 (March 1982).

2. For a discussion of the escape clause's failings, see Alan W. Wolff, "Need for New GATT Rules to Govern Safeguard Actions" in William R. Cline, ed., *Trade Policy in the 1980s* (Washington, D.C.: Institute for International Economics, 1983).

3. Section 201 is the successor to previous domestic statutes and executive orders. The original authority was provided under Executive Order 10082, which was superceded by section 7 of the Trade Agreements Extension Act of 1951. This gave way to section 301(b) of the Trade Expansion Act of 1962, which in turn was replaced by section 201 of the Trade Act of 1974.

4. The Office of the U.S. Trade Representative requested initiation of a specialty steel case in 1983, the 1977 and 1985 nonrubber footwear investigations were initiated at the request of the Senate Finance Committee, and the House Ways and Means Committee requested the initiation of an industrial fasteners investigation. All other escape-clause cases were initiated upon the petition of domestic industries.

5. The following departments, agencies, and councils are given an opportunity to participate in interagency discussions of escape-clause cases:

Department of Agriculture	Office of Management and
Department of Commerce	Budget
Department of Defense	Office of the U.S. Trade
Department of Energy	Representative
Department of Interior	Council of Economic
Department of Justice	Advisors
Department of Labor	National Security Council
Department of State	International Development
Department of Transportation	Cooperation Agency

The statute requires reports from the Department of Commerce and the Department of Labor stating how many firms and workers in the domestic industry are likely to be certified for adjustment assistance, and the extent to which their adjustment may be facilitated by existing programs.

6. See U.S. International Trade Commission, *Nonrubber Footwear; Report to the President on Investigation No. TA-201-50,* USITC Publication 1545 (July 1984).

7. When the commission finds that serious injury exists, it recommends relief to remedy the injury. If it finds the threat of injury, it recommends relief to prevent the injury.

8. See C. Michael Aho, "U.S. Labor-Market Adjustment and Import Restrictions" in Ernest H. Preeg, ed., *Hard Bargaining Ahead: U.S. Trade Policy and Developing Countries.* U.S.–Third World Policy Perspectives No. 4 (Washington, D.C.: Overseas Development Council, 1985).

9. A tariff-rate quota establishes different rates of duty at different import levels. For example, a tariff-rate quota could set a duty of $1 per widget for the first million imports, and $2 per widget thereafter.

10. Items 806.30 and 807 of the Tariff Schedules of the United States provide for partial duty exonerations on imported products that are assembled abroad from U.S. inputs. Imports under these two items only pay duty on the foreign value-added.

11. See U.S. International Trade Commission, *Nonrubber Footwear; Report to the President on Investigation No. TA-201-55*, USITC Publication 1717 (July 1985).

12. *Ibid.*

13. A case involving leather wearing apparel led to an override vote in the Senate, but this did not pass the House.

6
Countervailing and Antidumping Duties

The two principal forms of unfair trade practices are subsidization and dumping. Subsidies are direct or indirect government payments or benefits that are extended to producers or exporters of goods, while dumping consists of selling goods at less than fair value (LTFV). Both practices can distort market forces and injure the importing country's industries. U.S. trade law provides that subsidized or dumped imports may be answered with countervailing duties (CVDs) and antidumping duties (ADs), respectively.

These levies are not considered under the law to be punitive actions or instruments of import relief, but rather are intended to correct market distortions. Foreign exporters and domestic importers argue, however, that these remedies are often abused by protectionist industries, and that the laws give an unfair advantage to petitioners. Even unproven or trivial suits restrict access to the U.S. market by artificially raising the price of competition and creating uncertainty.

The Trade and Tariff Act of 1984 extensively amends the CVD and AD sections of the Tariff Act of 1930. Most amendments are intended to reduce and rationalize the work load of the administering agencies or to codify existing practices. Few of the amendments are radical departures from existing procedures, but their cumulative effect could be substantial. A number of changes work against the interests of respondents by widening the definition of unfair trade practices, facilitating the acceptance of petitions, easing the requirements for positive determinations, and facilitating retroactive imposition of penalties. Some of the provisions may work in favor of both respondents and petitioners by easing the procedural burdens imposed by the laws. A few may work in favor of respondents by reducing the level of dumping margins (the difference between an item's fair value and its U.S. price) in some cases, and by allowing the termination of existing CVD and AD duties in more situations.

U.S. Trade-Remedy Laws and the GATT

The development of modern U.S. trade-remedy laws dates back to the Tariff Act of 1897 (the Dingley Tariff), which provided for additional duties to be levied against imports that benefited from bounties or grants (that is, subsidies). This law only applied to dutiable imports, and did not require any proof that the bounty or grant in question led to the injury of a U.S. industry. The first U.S. antidumping statute was enacted in 1916, and was amended in 1921. Both the AD and CVD laws were codified in the Tariff Act of 1930 (the Smoot–Hawley Tariff), which to this day remains the basic antisubsidy and antidumping law of the United States. It has been significantly amended over the past half century, most notably by the Trade Act of 1974, the Trade Agreements Act of 1979, and the Trade and Tariff Act of 1984.

Since the negotiation of the General Agreement on Tariffs and Trade (GATT) in the 1940s, U.S. trade-remedy law has developed in tandem with GATT law. The GATT has attempted to establish some semblance of uniformity in the trade-remedy practices of its member countries, but its achievements in this regard have been mixed. GATT law on remedies for unfair trade practices has developed through several agreements, including articles VI and XVI of the General Agreement, the Antidumping Codes negotiated in the Kennedy and Tokyo Rounds, and the Tokyo Round's Code on Subsidies and Countervailing Duties (the Subsidies Code). These documents are by no means the last word on the subject, as the member states continue to differ over key questions such as the extension of the injury test, the definition of illegal subsidies, and special treatment for developing countries.

The Antidumping Code negotiated in the Kennedy Round MTN was the first GATT nontariff barrier code. Its purpose was to clarify and elaborate on the provisions of article VI of the GATT, establish procedural requirements for AD investigations, and bring all GATT signatories into conformity with article VI. Due to poor coordination between the executive and legislative branches, however, the United States never ratified the original code. The code was slightly revamped in the Tokyo Round negotiations and subsequently accepted by the United States. It entered into force for the United States on the same day as the revised U.S. antidumping statute (January 1, 1980).

The GATT Subsidies Code

The GATT Subsidies Code negotiated in the Tokyo Round has proven to be more controversial than the Antidumping Code, in part because subsidies are government policies rather than independent acts by private companies. Taking action against a foreign subsidy means, in effect, declaring that a foreign government has violated international trade law (as interpreted by the importing country). The code distinguishes between export subsidies, most of which are prohibited, and production (or domestic) subsidies. The latter are commonly extended in many industrialized and developing countries, and are not expressly prohibited under the code. Article XI of the code expressly recognizes that "subsidies other than export subsidies are widely used as important instruments for the promotion of social and economic policy objectives," such as the elimination of disadvantages borne by certain regions, the restructuring of economic sectors, sustaining employment and retraining programs, encouraging research and development, promoting economic development, and encouraging the redeployment of industry. The code does not strictly define or enumerate domestic subsidies, nor does it maintain that domestic subsidies are illegal, but it does enjoin signatories to seek to avoid causing injury to the industries of other signatories through the use of such subsidies.

The GATT Subsidies Code provides special consideration for developing countries. Part III of the code recognizes that "subsidies are an integral part of economic development programmes of developing countries," and the code does not prevent developing countries from adopting any subsidy which is consistent with its development and financial situation. The code only allows countermeasures against these subsidies if they prejudice the trade and production interests of other countries or result in the country capturing more than an equitable share of the world market.

The U.S. antisubsidy law incorporates the GATT Subsidies Code, but in many respects it establishes stricter standards. U.S. law stipulates that the export subsidy practices enumerated in the code's "Illustrative List of Export Subsidies" are subject to countervailing duties. The scope of U.S. law extends beyond the list, however, to cover any export subsidy, as well as domestic subsidies that are not generally available throughout the economy. For example, the code allows member countries to extend financing at below-market rates, as long as the rates are above those set by an international "gentleman's agreement" negotiated under the auspices of the Organization for Economic Cooperation and Development. In contrast, the United States views any subsidized financing to be subject to countervailing action. U.S. law has also been used to take action against agricultural subsidies, whereas the code normally does not prohibit subsidies on primary products.

The United States only applies the material injury test in CVD cases when the exporting country is "under the Agreement" (that is, adheres to the GATT Subsidies Code or assumes commitments to the United States substantially equivalent to code obligations). In most cases, the United States further requires that developing country signatories agree to eliminate or phase out their export subsidies as a condition for receiving the injury test. (Taiwan and Mexico are the only nonsignatories that have entered into bilateral undertakings that allow them to be considered under the agreement by the United States.) An exception to this rule is granted for seven small countries that prior to 1979 entered into treaties with the United States which required the United States to extend the injury test without conditions.[1] GATT members that are not signatories to the code are entitled to the injury test only in cases involving duty-free imports.

The extension of the injury test is an inducement for countries to accept GATT discipline and renounce export subsidies. This code reciprocity differs from the unconditional MFN principle that reigns in GATT law in that it establishes a prior condition that other countries must satisfy before receiving the treatment extended to a nation's most favored trading partners. For all practical purposes, these provisions eliminate any special treatment for less developed countries in U.S. antisubsidy law.

Although only a minority of GATT signatories adhere to the Subsidies Code, they are among the more important trading countries. The 21 signatories include the United States, the European Community, Japan, Canada, Hong Kong, India, Brazil, and South Korea.

The Domestic Politics of AD and CVD Laws

As we discussed in the introduction to this book, the rules of the game are an important arena in the fight over U.S. trade policy. From the perspective of some domestic industries, the trade-remedy laws have not kept up with developments in global practices. With the more blatant unfair trade practices being prohibited by international codes or domestic U.S. law, foreign exporters devise sophisticated means for promoting their exports and eluding these remedies. Self-styled reformers advocate making these practices subject to countervailing action. The major battles in the 98th Congress were fought over several novel proposals that would have vastly expanded the scope of U.S. trade-remedy laws. These initiatives would have made products subject to CVDs if they incorporated low-priced natural resources,[2] or to antidumping duties if they incorporated a component that had been sold at less than fair value in the producing country ("downstream dumping").[3] Another proposal would have established special rules for finding dumping on the part of "nonmarket economies" (communist countries),[4] while other bills would define industrial-targeting policies as unfair trade practices.

The Reagan administration and other advocates of liberal trade objected to these proposals. In addition to contesting the fairness, administrative feasibility, and economic wisdom of the laws, Secretary of Commerce Malcolm Baldrige and U.S. Trade Representative William Brock argued that many initiatives would violate international trade law.[5] The administration was also concerned that other countries would retaliate by enacting mirror legislation that would subject U.S. exports to the same rules in their markets. From the liberal trader's perspective, calls for the proverbial level playing field sometimes impose an unrealistic standard of fair trade on other countries—a standard which even the United States would be hard pressed to observe.

The U.S. trade-remedy laws were also criticized during the 98th Congress for their complexity and the costs they impose on domestic petitioners. There is no debating the point that trade-remedy proceedings are expensive undertakings for petitioners, respondents, and (indirectly) taxpayers. Parties to a trade-remedy case require the services of lawyers, accountants and other specialists. In order to be fair to both petitioners and respondents, the laws must provide the administering agencies with sufficient time to hear all arguments, collect and analyze information, and provide respondents a fair opportunity to respond to accusations about their practices.

Some of the proposals made during the 98th Congress would bring about real reforms by streamlining the laws and clarifying grey areas. Most of these initiatives were supported by the Reagan administration. The rapid increase in trade-remedy filings since 1981 and the increasingly complex legal procedures placed an overwhelming burden on the ITA and the USITC, and the executive branch sought easier mechanisms to conduct investigations, terminate proceedings, revoke existing AD or CVD orders, and reduce the number of judicial and administrative reviews. Other proposals made during the 98th Congress would have cut corners in the trade-remedy proceedings, often at the expense of respondents, by expediting some steps or eliminating preliminary findings. These initiatives were criticized as penny-wise and pound-foolish measures that would simply multiply the number of appeals made to the Court of International Trade (CIT)—thus increasing the long-run cost of trade-remedy proceedings for all parties.

The end result of the trade-remedy debate was title VI (Trade Law Reform) of the TTA, which extensively amends the CVD and AD laws. For the most part, the Reagan administration succeeded in defeating those proposals that it considered to be inconsistent with the GATT. The downstream dumping, natural resource subsidization, and nonmarket economy provisions were all rejected, while the industrial-targeting initiative was deflected by calling for further study. The TTA does include some restrictive sections, such as those covering upstream subsidies, cumulation of imports, and expanded requirements for the prosecution of "persistent dumping," but they are much less comprehensive than many of the original proposals that were dropped. Some of the reforms that were favored by the administration are also included in title VI.

Flow of Trade-Remedy Proceedings

An overview of the trade-remedy process is in order before describing the details of the laws and the changes made by the 1984 amendments.

The International Trade Administration of the Commerce Department (ITA), acting on behalf of the Secretary of Commerce, has concurrent responsibility with the USITC for the administration of the AD and CVD laws. The ITA is charged with determining the existence and the amount of any subsidy or dumping margin, negotiating any agreements intended to offset these practices, imposing duties, reviewing the effectiveness of the remedy, and determining when to terminate or modify any remedy.

The USITC applies an injury test to determine whether subsidized or dumped imports cause or threaten material injury to domestic parties, or retard the establishment of a domestic industry. This injury test is automatic in AD cases, but is extended in CVD cases only when the country meets certain conditions. If the country is not entitled to the injury test, then the ITA has sole control over the proceedings. If the injury test is applied, then both agencies must reach positive determinations in order for an antidumping or countervailing duty to be ordered against the foreign exporter.

The procedures followed in most AD and CVD cases are illustrated in figures 6–1 and 6–2. In a typical case, ten months or more will elapse between the time a proceeding begins and when any assessment of duties against imports is made. Proceedings begin when a petition is filed with the USITC and the ITA by an interested party on behalf of an industry, or may be initiated by the ITA on its own motion. When the petition is filed by an interested party, the ITA has twenty days to determine whether the petition is sufficient for the initiation of an investigation.

The determination regarding the sufficiency of a petition is made on the basis of the evidence presented by the petitioner. A petition must set out a *prima facie* case, meaning that it must include the requisite information needed for the ITA to pursue a case. If the ITA finds that the evidence appears to warrant an investigation, the commission begins its investigation. The USITC has forty-five days after the filing of a petition to reach a preliminary determination as to whether there is a "reasonable indication" of material injury. The commission allows all parties to the investigation to submit briefs prior to issuing this preliminary determination, and may also hold a conference on the matter. A negative determination by the USITC at this stage will terminate the proceedings, although the low empirical threshold set by the "reasonable indication" standard makes preliminary negative decisions rare.[6]

If the USITC's preliminary determination is affirmative, the ITA is informed and continues its investigation. In the ITA's preliminary determination, it must find whether there is a reasonable basis to believe that the foreign producer is engaging in the unfair trade practice. Commerce Department investigators send questionnaires to foreign and domestic parties requesting financial and other information, and (usually at a later stage of the investigation) verify the responses through on-site visits and audits. Foreign producers may refuse to provide information or allow verification by the ITA, but do so at their own risk. The ITA will proceed on the basis of the best information available, including that supplied by the petitioner. It is not uncommon for the ITA to levy much higher duties on foreign producers that did not supply information than it does on those who cooperated.

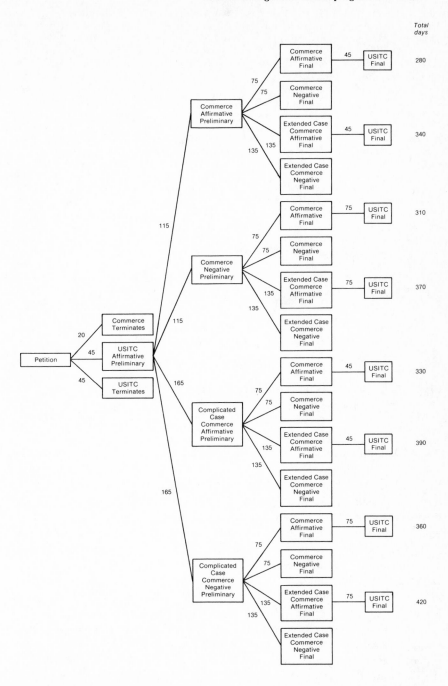

Figure 6–1. Statutory Timetable for Antidumping Investigations (in days)

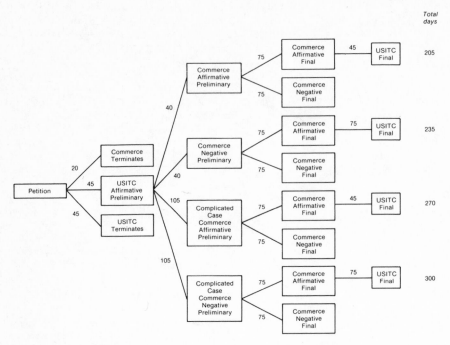

Figure 6–2. Statutory Timetable for Countervailing Duty Investigations (in days)

A preliminary affirmative decision leads to the announcement of a preliminary margin, notification of the USITC, and an order to the Customs Service that a cash deposit be made or a bond posted for each entry, pending resolution of the proceedings. The Customs Service will also suspend the liquidation or final assessment of duties on any future entries. The deposit or bond must be equal to the preliminary margin found by the ITA. Even though deposits or bonds will be refunded if the final determinations are negative, the costs of posting the security and the uncertainty created by these circumstances may encourage importers or their customers to seek other sources of supply. If the ITA reaches a preliminary negative determination, the proceedings continue, but imports may still enter without any required securities.

The ITA carries on with its investigation, whether its preliminary determination was affirmative or negative. If the final ITA finding is negative, the proceedings are terminated by both the ITA and the USITC. If it is positive, then the ITA must determine a dumping or subsidy margin that may be less than, equal to, or greater than the preliminary margin.

Following an affirmative final determination by the ITA, the USITC holds a formal hearing in which all interested parties participate. If the commission's final determination is affirmative, then the ITA issues antidumping or counter-vailing duty orders against the imported merchandise. The orders are equal to the final margin found by the ITA, and usually require deposits of estimated duties for the next twelve-month period. If the commission's final determination is negative, then the case terminates and any securities posted after the preliminary determinations are returned.

This schedule assumes no unusual procedures or rulings. At the request of the petitioner or on its own motion, the ITA may decide in "extraordinarily complicated cases" to postpone its preliminary determination. The ITA also has the authority to conduct expedited reviews in certain cases.

If the petitioner withdraws the petition before the final determinations are announced, the ITA or the USITC will terminate the proceedings. These with-drawals often result from the ITA settling cases "out of court" with the foreign government, or the exporters agreeing to take steps that appease the petitioner. The ITA may also reach suspension agreements that freeze cases at some stage in the process without the imposition of a CVD or AD duty. If a suspension agreement is violated, it may be reopened at the stage where it had been suspended.

Once ordered, antidumping and countervailing duties remain in place until revoked. The ITA reviews orders and suspension agreements on an annual basis, and if the circumstances warrant it, the ITA may revive a suspended investiga-tion or adjust the rate of duty. The ITA and the USITC will also consider requests to review changed circumstances in order to determine whether to revoke an outstanding order or terminate a suspension agreement.

The Court of International Trade has jurisdiction over the trade-remedy laws, with appellate authority resting with the Court of Appeals for the Federal Circuit. Both petitioners and respondents may appeal to the CIT.

Antidumping and antisubsidy cases have become an increasingly important focus of U.S. trade relations, as the number of petitions filed in recent years has grown dramatically. The high-water mark came in fiscal year 1982, when the U.S. steel industry filed 144 petitions against foreign competitors. From fiscal years 1982 through the first half of 1985, the industry filed 241 petitions alleging that foreign producers sold steel at less than fair value in the U.S. market or benefited from illegal subsidies.

Table 6–1 shows USITC and ITA activity in AD and CVD cases during 1984. A total of 125 petitions were filed that year. Eighty-one investigations were completed, including many that began in 1983. Twenty-nine case termi-nated when negative determinations were reached by either the USITC or the ITA, and 36 new AD and CVD orders were issued. Twenty-one cases led to suspensions, withdrawals, or terminations of petitions, and 18 existing orders were revoked. At year's end, 108 AD orders and 53 CVD orders were in effect.

Table 6–1
Summary of Antidumping and Countervailing Duty Cases in 1984

	AD	CVD	Total
Petitions filed	73	52	125
Investigations completed	49	32	81
Negative determinations			
Preliminary USITC	4	3	7
Final ITA	5	6	11
Final USITC	9	2	11
Affirmative determinations			
Final ITA	38	18	56
Final USITC	19	5	24
Suspensions of investigations	0	3	3
Withdrawal or termination of petitions	13	6	19
Final AD or CVD orders	22	14	36
Revocations of old orders	10	8	18
Total orders in place as of December 31, 1984	108	53	161

Source: Adapted from U.S. International Trade Commission, *Operation of the Trade Agreements Program*, 36th annual report, USITC Publication 1725 (July 1985), pp. 197–99, 236–45.

More detail on these 161 orders is given in table 6–2. The orders are issued against imports from 32 different countries, but just 8 countries account for 101 of them. Most of the orders were issued from 1980 to 1984, but some were issued as long ago as 1963. The duty rate on these orders ranges from a fraction of a percent to over 100 percent.

Initiation of Cases

Trade-remedy cases are initiated upon the filing of petitions by interested parties on behalf of an industry or by the ITA on its own motion. The USITC cannot initiate cases. The Tariff Act of 1930 provides that an "interested party" is a producer, a union or other group of workers, or a trade or business association. The interested party must produce a "like product" in order to have standing under the trade-remedy statutes.

Legal Standing for Coalitions

The act extends the right of petition to coalitions of U.S. companies, trade associations, and labor unions. Earlier, in the case of *Matsushita Electrical Co. v. United States* (1983), the Court of International Trade had found that an ad hoc coalition of labor and industry groups did not have standing before the USITC because not all of its members had such standing individually. Under section 612(b)(2) of the TTA, petitions may be submitted by "an association, a majority of whose members is composed of interested parties." This effectively reverses the CIT's *Matsushita* decision. The provision favors petitioners over

Table 6-2
Countervailing Duty and Antidumping
Orders In Effect as of December 31, 1984

Country	ADs	CVDs	Total
Japan	33	2	35
Mexico	1	11	12
Canada	10	0	10
Brazil	5	4	9
France	8	1	9
South Korea	6	3	9
Spain	1	8	9
Argentina	2	6	8
Italy	7	1	8
Taiwan	7	0	7
West Germany	6	1	7
People's Republic of China	5	0	5
Sweden	4	1	5
South Africa	0	4	4
United Kingdom	1	2	3
Australia	1	1	2
Finland	2	0	2
Peru	0	2	2
Trinidad and Tobago	1	1	2
Austria	1	0	1
Belgium	1	0	1
Chile	1	0	1
Dominican Republic	1	0	1
East Germany	1	0	1
European Community	0	1	1
Israel	0	1	1
Netherlands	1	0	1
Pakistan	0	1	1
Philippines	0	1	1
U.S.S.R.	1	0	1
Uruguay	0	1	1
Yugoslavia	1	0	1
Total	108	53	161

Source: Adapted from U.S. International Trade Commission, *Operation of the Trade Agreements Program*, 36th annual report, USITC Publication 1725 (July 1985), pp. 236–45.

respondents, as it allows coalitions to include more politically influential members than they otherwise could, and to share the legal costs among a larger group.

Standing for Wine Grape Growers

The requirement that a petitioner produce a "like product" is complicated when a trade-remedy case centers on inputs that are used to produce a finished product. This is particularly true for agricultural goods that undergo processing between the farmer and the consumer. The Congress anticipated the difficulties in defining a domestic industry by allowing the USITC to consider both growers and producers to be a single industry when the conditions warrant it. The commission has used its discretion cautiously. When the agricultural product is exclusively produced for a single processing industry, the USITC ordinarily considers the growers and the processors to be integrated into a single industry for purposes of trade-remedy cases.

A coalition of wine grape growers from New York and California filed CVD and AD petitions against Italian and French wines in January 1984. The USITC reached a negative preliminary decision two months later. The commission's decision was based on the absence of causation between imports and any injury that the domestic industry might be experiencing. The USITC also determined that the wine grape growers did not have legal standing. Because grapes can be sold for other purposes, such as table grapes or raisins, the USITC found that there was not a sufficient degree of integration between the growers and the wineries for the former to have standing.[7]

The grape growers simultaneously appealed the commission's decision before the Court of International Trade, and urged the Congress to change the trade-remedy laws in a way that would favor their cause. The grape growers' legislative proposal would have given standing in cases involving any processed agricultural products to "the producers of that product and the producers of the principal raw agricultural product." This proposal was opposed by the European Community, the Reagan administration, and U.S. agricultural exporters who feared that it would spark European retaliation against their products. The Congress responded to these concerns by limiting the extended definition of like products to growers of wine grapes.

Under section 612 of the TTA, the wine industry is defined to include "the domestic producers of the principal raw agricultural product ... which is included in the like domestic product, if those producers allege material injury, or threat of material injury, as a result of imports of such wine and grape products." This special dispensation only lasts through October 30, 1986.

Even though the provision was limited to growers of wine grapes, it still provoked a dispute with the EC. The European representatives to the GATT requested formal dispute-settlement proceedings, but the United States protested that the issue was moot unless and until the law is actually employed in a proceeding that leads to the imposition of countervailing or antidumping duties. As of this writing, the point is still in dispute. The CIT later ruled that the USITC was correct in denying standing to the grape growers, but overturned the commission's finding that there was no reasonable indication of material injury. The USITC responded by appealing the CIT's decision before the Court of Appeals for the Federal Circuit.

The growers hesitated to use the TTA provision to file a new petition until their appeal of the 1984 case was resolved, but the prospects of a prolonged court battle between the CIT and the USITC discouraged the growers from relying solely on this course of action. They filed a new set of AD and CVD petitions in September 1985, which led to a second negative determination by the USITC.[8]

Self-Initiated ITA Investigations of Persistent Dumping

Section 609 of the act facilitates self-initiation of dumping investigations by the ITA in cases of "persistent dumping" that involve more than one country. The law provides that the ITA may monitor the imports of a class or kind of merchandise from any supplier country for up to one year if more than one antidumping order is in effect, if there is reason to believe or suspect an "extraordinary pattern of persistent injurious dumping" from one or more additional supplier countries, and if the ITA believes that this extraordinary pattern is causing a serious commercial problem for the domestic industry.

The initial application of this provision is discretionary, but the ITA must self-initiate an AD investigation if it determines in the course of this monitoring that there is sufficient cause to do so. According to the language, the ITA "may" choose to begin monitoring a given product, but if it finds sufficient evidence, it "shall" begin an investigation.

This provision might encourage the ITA to use its power of self-initiation more frequently. The ITA will now be under more pressure to monitor and self-initiate when the circumstances appear to warrant it, and these circumstances may be subject to manipulation. Domestic industries will be tempted to win a few easy victories over small suppliers in order to press the Department of Commerce into monitoring the imports of the same product from other countries. If this monitoring leads to self-initiation by the ITA, then the domestic industries will have succeeded in bringing action against several competitors without bearing the full legal costs themselves. Monitoring might also establish a certain expectation of guilt on the part of the suppliers in question. The domestic groups that supported this provision, however, are concerned that the ITA will not actually utilize it in many cases, and that they still must bear the legal costs of participating in any proceedings that may be initiated. The provision falls short of their original proposal, in which preliminary affirmative findings would have been automatic.

Trade-Remedy Assistance Center

Several industry groups voiced their concern during the 98th Congress that the trade-remedy laws are beyond the reach of small-scale enterprises that allegedly suffer from unfair foreign competition. Cost estimates for the legal fees and other expenses range from $100,000 to $1 million, which is well beyond the means of most small businesses, and the sheer complexity of the laws keeps many potential petitioners from filing.[9] Several proposals for assisting small businesses were aired during the 98th Congress, including creation of a small business advocate within the Department of Commerce to help small businesses pursue trade remedies, fast-track provisions that would eliminate some steps in AD and CVD proceedings, and even cash grants to small businesses to defray the costs of pursuing import relief.

In lieu of establishing an advocate in the Department of Commerce, the Congress created an advisor within the USITC. Section 221 of the TTA establishes a new Trade Remedy Assistance Center whose stated purpose is to provide full information to the public on the remedies and benefits available under the trade laws, and petition and application procedures.[10] The act makes no provision for self-initiation of cases by this center, and the USITC has isolated the center from the rest of the commission so as to avoid crossing the fine line between advice and advocacy.

The TTA also extends some assistance to qualifying small businesses by directing each agency responsible for administering a trade law (principally the USITC, the ITA, and the USTR) to "provide technical assistance to eligible small businesses to enable them to prepare and file petitions and applications." According to the law, "eligible small businesses" include any business concern that "has neither adequate internal resources nor financial ability to obtain qualified outside assistance in preparing and filing petitions and applications" under these laws. The agencies had previously extended such assistance informally, and without explicit legislative guidance.

Petitions involving Sales

Section 602 of the act clarifies that petitions may be filed in cases involving sales as well as actual importations. Sales are defined to include irrevocable offers to sell, other "likely sales," and leasing arrangements that are equivalent to sales. The previous law did not explicitly cover products that are sold but not yet imported into the United States, or products that are subject to a leasing arrangement. In a case involving railcars from Canada, however, a countervailing duty was ordered against imports benefiting from subsidized export financing.[11] The injury to U.S. producers was caused in this case by the loss of the bid, which occurred well before the actual importation into the United States. The railcar precedent is now codified by the TTA.

Injury Investigations of the USITC

Material injury occurs when the imports under investigation in a trade-remedy case cause or threaten to cause material injury to a U.S. industry, or retard the establishment of an industry. Material injury is defined by the Tariff Act of 1930 (as amended) as "harm which is not inconsequential, immaterial, or unimportant."

The law specifies that the USITC is to take into account three key considerations (volume, price, and impact) in determining whether this harm has been done. In evaluating the volume of imports, the commission considers whether "any increase in that volume, either in absolute terms or relative to production or consumption in the United States, is significant." In evaluating the effect that imports have on prices, the commission looks for "significant price undercutting" by the imported merchandise as compared with the price of like products in the United States, and whether imports depress prices or prevent price increases. The impact on a domestic industry is assessed by evaluating "all relevant economic factors which have a bearing on the state of the industry," such as production, employment, market share, profits, and wages.

Criteria for the Threat of Material Injury

Until the passage of the TTA, the USITC had no statutory guidelines for determining when a domestic industry is faced with the threat of material injury (as distinct from actually experiencing material injury). This created uncertainty in those cases where the USITC came short of finding the existence of material injury, but believed that material injury was threatened. Opinions differed among trade lawyers as to whether the legislative history of the Trade Agreements Act of 1979 provided the commissioners with sufficient guidance in such cases.[12]

Section 612 codifies the commission's understanding of what constitutes a threat of material injury. The threat of injury may be indicated by increases in production capacity or existing unused capacity in the exporting country, rapid increases in U.S. market penetration, import prices that will have a depressing or suppressing effect on domestic prices, substantial increases in U.S. inventories, the presence of underutilized capacity in the exporting country, and the potential for product shifting. All but the last of these indicators were already cited in the legislative history of the trade-remedy statutes. The conference report further emphasizes that any determination must be based on evidence that the threat is real and that actual injury is imminent. Mere supposition and conjecture are not sufficient cause for a determination.

Cumulation in the Determination of Material Injury

The act sets out additional criteria that the USITC must weigh when determining whether an unfair trade practice causes or threatens material injury for a U.S. industry. The most important of these additions concerns the "cumulation" of suppliers in CVD and AD cases. As noted above, the volume of imports is one of the three principal considerations that the USITC must currently take into account when determining whether the imports cause material injury to U.S. industry. If volume is only examined country-by-country, then the imports under investigation are less likely to comprise a significant share of the domestic market.

Prior to the TTA, the commissioners had the discretion to cumulate the imports of more than one country. This decision was made on a case-by-case basis and was not governed by specific legislative guidance. Among the criteria used by the commissioners in deciding whether or not to cumulate were the degree of fungibility between imports from various countries and the domestic like product, the existence of common or similar channels of distribution, geographic concentration of the imports and the like domestic product, whether the prices of imports and the domestic like product were within a reasonable range, and whether the imports were simultaneously present in the market. Commissioners could decide not to cumulate imports from countries whose market share was considered to be too small to be a "contributing cause" of injury to the domestic industry.

Section 612 of the TTA eliminates the contributing-cause standard. Under the new language, countries with even miniscule market shares must be cumulated if three criteria are met: the products must compete with other imports and the like product in the domestic market, they must be marketed within a reasonably coincidental period, and they must be under investigation. This three-step test clearly reduces the commission's discretion in deciding whether to cumulate, and works against the interest of smaller suppliers who might have escaped under the contributing-cause test. For example, in early 1985, the USITC applied the mandatory cumulation rule in a case involving oil country tubular goods (OCTG). Even though these suppliers each had an average market share of less than 1 percent during the period under investigation, the commissioners felt compelled to cumulate their imports. The resulting preliminary affirmative finding for each of the countries might not have been made if the suppliers were not cumulated.[13]

The legislation leaves some questions unanswered, and these must be addressed by evolving USITC practice. One important issue is how to deal with CVD cases involving some producers that are entitled to an injury test and others that are not. The commission still has it within its discretion to cumulate products from countries that are not entitled to an injury test. Section 612 of the TTA only requires that imports currently under investigation be included in the cumulation. The USITC does not usually investigate the products without an injury test because the question of injury has no effect on them. Even if the USITC does not find injury, the countries that are not entitled to an injury test would be subject to the CVD necessary to offset the subsidy margin found by ITA.

Another problem area is the issue of cross-cumulation, meaning the cumulation of products in a CVD case with like products in a pending AD case (or vice versa). A majority of the present commissioners apparently believe that cross-cumulation is inappropriate.

Investigations by the ITA

The TTA modifies the definitions and proceedings followed by the ITA in antidumping and antisubsidy proceedings.

Dumping Investigations

The ITA must establish whether and by what degree the imports under investigation are sold at less than fair value. Dumping occurs when the fair value of the product exceeds the price of the imported product in the United States (the U.S. price). This apparently straightforward calculus is complicated by numerous possible variations on the theme. Depending on the circumstances involved in a particular case, any one of several values can be used in the equation "fair value minus U.S. price equals the dumping margin."

Fair value (also called foreign market value) may be the price at which the product is sold in the foreign producer's home market, the price at which it is exported to another country, or a constructed value calculated from production costs. When the U.S. importer and the foreign exporter are not related, the U.S. price is the price at which the merchandise is purchased prior to the date of importation from a foreign producer for export to the U.S. market (purchase price). When the U.S. importer and the foreign exporter are related parties (for example, when one is a subsidiary of the other), the U.S. price is the exporter's sales price, or the price at which the merchandise is sold or agreed to be sold to the first unrelated purchaser in the United States.

Foreign Market Value. The TTA redefines the time at which foreign market value is determined in those cases where the U.S. price is based on the exporter's sales price. The definition is changed from the "price at the time of exportation" to the price in the home market at the time the merchandise is first sold to an unrelated purchaser in the United States. This redefinition could have restrictive consequences. Because the price of goods tends to increase over time, and would thus lead to a higher fair market value, there is the likelihood of a slightly higher dumping margin under the new definition.

Reseller. The ITA must determine in some cases the country that will be used as the home market for calculating foreign market value. This determination can be complicated when the merchandise passes through several hands before reaching the United States. Section 614 of the TTA states that in those cases, the foreign market value is the appropriate price in the home market of the reseller.

Adjustments Study. In determining the U.S. price and/or the foreign market value, the ITA may take into account various adjustments in order to assure comparability. These complicating factors include import or export taxes, the cost of packing and shipping goods, the amount of any countervailing duty already imposed by the United States or export subsidies bestowed on the merchandise, and allowances for the circumstances of sale, quantity discounts, and quality differences. The ITA's use of adjustments has evolved over several decades, and has been the subject of criticism from both petitioners and respondents. The dispute resurfaced following a 1982 finding concerning typewriters from Japan, in which the adjustments made by the ITA investigators eliminated any dumping margin. The Court of International Trade upheld the ITA's decision, but the ensuing controversy led the Congress to investigate the role of adjustments in antidumping proceedings.

Section 624 of the TTA calls for the Department of Commerce to undertake a study of the use of adjustments when determining the foreign market value and U.S. price of a product. The report is to focus on types of adjustments currently being made, the manner and extent to which such adjustments have led to inequitable results, and private sector comments and recommendations made at the congressional hearings during the 98th Congress. The report will include recommendations "regarding the need, and the means, for simplifying and modifying current practices in the making of such adjustments." The study could form the basis of new initiatives to amend the AD statute.

Sampling and Averaging. The act significantly expands the ITA's authority to employ sampling and averaging techniques in AD investigations and annual reviews. Under the previous practice, the ITA could use these methods to arrive at a weighted average price for each foreign seller when determining foreign market value in AD cases. The resulting foreign market value was then compared to the U.S. price for each sale to find out which sales, if any, were made at prices lower than their market value. The calculation was biased by the ITA practice of not including any sales for which the price was above the market value.

Section 620 of the act extends the sampling and averaging authority to the determination of the U.S. price for each exporter. This will only be done when an investigation covers a "significant" number of sales or when a "significant" number of price adjustments is required; the legislation does not define *significant*. Under previous practice, U.S. sales prices above the foreign market value were ignored in the ITA's calculations, but now they can be included in the average. To the extent that this occurs, the average U.S. price may tend to be higher, and dumping findings may be less numerous or margins may tend to be smaller.

Subsidy Investigations

The Tariff Act of 1930 (as amended) provides that any export subsidy may be subject to CVDs. Domestic subsidies may also be answered with countervailing action if they are "provided or required by government action to a specific enterprise or industry," whether they are "paid or bestowed directly or indirectly on the manufacture, production or export of any class or kind of merchandise." As examples of such domestic subsidies, the law cites the provision of capital, loans, or loan guarantees on below-market terms, the provision of goods or services at preferential rates, debt forgiveness, and the assumption of any costs or expenses of manufacture, production, or distribution. As a general rule, the United States will consider any subsidy to be potentially subject to countervailing duties if it benefits an exporter and is not generally available to all industries in the exporter's home country.

Upstream Subsidization. Section 613 of the act adds "upstream subsidization" to the list of prohibited subsidies against which the United States may apply CVDs. These subsidies are not dealt with in the GATT Subsidies Code or the Tariff Act of 1930, but developed on its own as an ITA investigative practice. An upstream subsidy is granted to one of the principal components used in the product under investigation. The ITA had previously considered the existence of upstream subsidies in cases where European steel mills were alleged to benefit from subsidies on coking coal and European pasta producers benefited from a subsidy on wheat.[14] Title VI of the TTA codifies the ITA methods with some embellishment.

Some critics argue that the upstream subsidy approach violates GATT norms. The respondents in a case involving agricultural tillage tools from Brazil argued that upstream subsidies should be subject to countervailing duties only if the benefits are specifically directed at the downstream producers. This argument reflected the well-established principle that subsidies are not subject to CVDs when they are generally available throughout the economy. Because the subsidized steel was generally available to producers in Brazil, and not produced specifically for the benefit of the farm implement industry, the respondents argued that no upstream subsidy should be found. If this position were accepted, it would definitely limit the applicability of the upstream subsidy provision. The ITA disagreed, however, arguing that nothing in the statute or its legislative history supported this contention.[15]

The TTA requires the ITA to investigate upstream subsidies whenever it has "reasonable grounds to believe or suspect" that such a subsidy is bestowed, whether the subsidy is provided by a single government or a customs union. The legislation establishes three tests that the ITA must apply in order to find an upstream subsidy. First, the law stipulates that the subsidy on the input must be bestowed on an input that is "used in the manufacture or production in that country of merchandise which is the subject of a countervailing duty proceeding." This rules out the consideration of subsidies on imported inputs bestowed by third countries.

Second, the ITA must find that the subsidy "bestows a competitive benefit" on the finished product in order for the subsidy to be passed through. A competitive benefit is bestowed when the price for the input is lower than the price that the manufacturer or producer of the finished product would otherwise pay in obtaining it from another seller in an arms-length transaction. The procedures laid out by the TTA for determining the price a manufacturer would otherwise have to pay for the input differ from the ITA's previous, uncodified practice. The TTA methods require the ITA to adjust the comparison prices to reflect any known subsidies, while the earlier ITA practice made no allowance for such adjustments. By allowing investigators to factor in these "subsidies once-removed," this provision could increase the calculated level of subsidization.

Finally, the ITA must determine whether the upstream subsidy "has a significant effect on the cost of manufacturing or producing" the end products. The legislation does not define what is meant by significant. In the ITA's preliminary determination in the Brazilian case, the investigators somewhat arbitrarily took this to mean that the estimated net subsidy must account for more than 1 percent of the cost of manufacturing or producing the merchandise. In the final determination, however, the ITA rejected this 1-percent threshold as an inappropriate measure of the effect that an upstream subsidy has on the competitiveness of finished goods.[16] In place of a rigid 1-percent standard, the ITA established a range of between 1 and 5 percent. Any calculated subsidy below 1 percent would lead to a presumption of no significant effect, while subsidies above 5 percent would lead the ITA to presume a significant effect. This range is not immutable; the ITA will take into consideration any evidence suggesting that a higher or lower threshold would be appropriate in a particular case.

Congress recognized the complexities of upstream subsidization, and the law therefore specifies that the time limits for determinations in cases involving alleged upstream subsidization can be extended. However, suspension of liquidation will not continue more than four months between the preliminary and final determinations. This proviso was required in order to keep the law consistent with the GATT Subsidies Code's requirements on the duration of provisional measures.

As of this writing, the ITA has not yet taken action against an upstream subsidy under the authority of the TTA. One case involving Mexican paper products was withdrawn prior to a final determination, while the Brazilian farm implements case changed course in midstream. The latter case yielded a 0.71-percent upstream subsidy in the preliminary determination (accounting for a fraction of the 4.33-percent net subsidy), a figure that was revised to 1.14 percent in the final determination. The ITA determined that this level of subsidy did not have a significant effect on the competitiveness of Brazilian tillage tools, and therefore did not include the upstream subsidy in its final subsidy margin of 8.06 percent.

Industrial-Targeting Study. *Targeting* is the coordination of government assistance to specific industries in order to make them competitive in the international market. It may take the form of research and development assistance, protection of the home market from import competition, below-market financing, subsidization of production, and export promotion. The classic example of targeting is Japanese assistance to its high technology industries, but several industrialized and developing countries pursue similar policies.[17]

Targeting has been denounced by several U.S. businesses as their single most insuperable obstacle to competing in the world marketplace. They claim that while their products can compete with those of any rival in the private sector, they cannot hope to win when their competitors are backed by the full force of their governments. Viewing targeting as the ultimate form of government intervention in the market, they argue that it should be declared an unfair trade practice that is subject to U.S. retaliation.

Legislation was introduced in the 98th Congress that would make industrial targeting a prohibited subsidy under the U.S. CVD statute. In closely examining the issue, however, the Congress discovered the enormous practical difficulties that arise in the targeting issue. First, the very definition of unfair targeting is problematic. Nearly all modern governments employ some policies that might be construed as targeting, such as the U.S. government's patronage of the domestic aerospace and defense industries. This in turn leads to the question of retaliation; if the United States unilaterally penalized foreign producers who benefit from targeting, would other countries take similar action against U.S. producers?

Rather than decide the issue immediately, the TTA remanded it for further study. In section 625 of the TTA, Congress commissioned a set of industrial targeting studies to be prepared individually by the ITA, the USTR, the Department of Labor, and the General Accounting Office. The studies were to focus on "whether foreign industrial targeting should be considered as an unfair trade practice under United States law," and whether current laws, including the CVD statute, "adequately address the subsidy element of foreign industrial policy measures." The proposal called for the investigating agencies to include in their reports "any recommended legislation considered necessary based on the study results."

None of the studies suggested the need for major reforms in the trade-remedy statutes. For example, the General Accounting Office concluded that "current U.S. trade law, particularly section 301 and the countervailing duty statutes, have the capability to address instances when foreign industrial targeting is judged to unfairly affect trade."[18] The only legislative change recommended by the USTR was an alteration in section 102 of the Trade Act of 1974, under which the executive branch may submit trade agreements on nontariff matters to the Congress for fast-track ratification (see chapter 2). The USTR recommended that the 1974 act be amended to authorize the USTR to offer U.S. concessions in exchange for the elimination of foreign acts, policies, and practices that are legally fair, but that restrict U.S. exports and are likely to enhance the foreign industry's competitiveness to the detriment of U.S.

producers.[19] This change would presumably give the USTR the ability to negotiate modifications in the targeting schemes used by U.S. trading partners.

These studies may not have discouraged Capitol Hill from limiting the executive's discretion in dealing with industrial targeting issues. During the 99th Congress, many proposals were floated to amend the statutes. Some initiatives would make industrial targeting subject to mandatory retaliation under section 301 (if the USITC found it to cause injury to U.S. industry), while others would require the USITC to consider targeting policies to be an indicator of serious injury under the escape clause, or direct the Department of Commerce to establish a special office to monitor and investigate foreign targeting practices.

Additional Rules, Procedures, and Definitions

Simultaneous AD/CVD Investigations and Hearings. Prior to the TTA, CVD and AD cases were considered in separate investigations on separate timetables, even if they concerned identical products from the same countries. This presented problems for both petitioners and respondents. The domestic industry with a legitimate grievance was burdened by the substantial legal costs involved in seeking redress under distinct proceedings. The obverse was also true: some domestic industries abused the right to file multiple petitions, and harassed their foreign competition by forcing them to devote considerable time and resources to several proceedings at the same time.

Section 606 of the TTA provides that where AD and CVD cases are simultaneously initiated on imports of the same product and from the same countries, the petitioner can request that the deadline for CVD findings be delayed to coincide with the due date for the AD final determination. As in the case of upstream subsidization, the suspension of liquidation cannot remain in place between the preliminary and final determinations for more than 120 days.

Section 616 of the act provides for simultaneous hearings. When CVD and AD investigations are initiated within six months of one another and involve the same merchandise from the same country, the USITC may hold a single hearing for both investigations. The commissioners may still hold separate hearings if they find that special circumstances require them to do so.

These provisions will relieve both petitioners and respondents of part of their legal burdens, but they are also open to potential abuse. Because it will now be easier for domestic interests to pursue relief under both the CVD and AD procedures, this rule could encourage duplicate petitions that might not otherwise be filed.

Critical Circumstances. Foreign exporters sometimes attempt to export large quantities of a product before an AD or CVD case is settled so that they can avoid paying the extra duties that might be levied on future shipments. When the petitioner alleges that exporters are trying to beat the imposition of the duty, the ITA is directed to determine whether critical circumstances are present. These circumstances occur when there have been massive imports over a short period of time. In subsidy cases, the ITA must also determine that the export subsidy was in violation of the code. In dumping cases, the ITA must further determine that there is a history of dumping or that the importer knew of the sales at less than fair value. In final determination the U.S. ITC must also make a finding that the massive imports found by the ITA were the cause of material injury. If critical circumstances are found, then the ITA must direct that the suspension of liquidation and the posting of security apply retroactively to unliquidated entries that were entered or withdrawn from warehouse ninety days prior to an existing suspension order.

The new legislation clarifies this provision by providing that critical circumstances may be found in the final CVD or AD determination, even though the preliminary ITA determination on the existence of a subsidy was negative. In such a case, the suspension and security requirements for unliquidated entries apply to ninety days before the final determination. The ITA may also find critical circumstance in the final determination if the preliminary determination was positive, but indicated no critical circumstance. In this case, the suspension and security requirements apply to ninety days before the preliminary determination for unliquidated entries. This works against the interests of foreign exporters as it lengthens the period during which they are in jeopardy of such a finding.

Treatment of Confidential Information. Section 619 of the TTA streamlines the procedures for the submission, acceptance, summarization, and release under protective order of confidential information that is gathered during the course of a proceeding. Prior to the TTA, such information could be released only to the staffs of the ITA and the USITC. This created contentious arguments and legal proceedings in some cases. The TTA permits the release of confidential information to officers of the U.S. Customs Service in fraud investigations, and to private importers under protective order. The TTA also replaces the term *confidential* with the more flexible phrase *proprietary business information,* in order to avoid confusion with the term *confidential* as used by the national security community.

Verification of Information. Section 603 of the TTA allows the parties to waive the verification of information collected during a CVD investigation; there was already a parallel provision in the AD statute. Provided that the ITA and all parties to the investigation agree, a preliminary determination may be made without verification of the information which the ITA has collected. This is a noncontroversial measure that offers equal benefits to petitioners and respondents by allowing them to shorten the length of the preliminary phase by mutual consent.

Commercial Quantities. The TTA replaces the phrase *wholesale quantities* with the phrase *commercial quantities* in CVD and AD investigations. The reference to *wholesale* might have erroneously been interpreted to mean a level or class of sale, rather than refering to its size.

Proceedings. The previous statute required that the ITA and the USITC include in their CVD investigations any subsidies that are discovered in the course of those investigations. The TTA extends this requirement to any subsidies discovered in the course of the "proceedings." A "proceeding" begins with the initial filing of a petition, and continues until revocation or termination. It is more comprehensive than an "investigation," which only covers the period when the ITA is actually carrying out its investigations.

Suspension and Termination

Congress did not provide the executive branch with extensive discretion on the administration of the AD and CVD laws. Unlike section 301, which is entirely subject to executive discretion (see chapter 2), and section 201, which allows the White House to accept, reject, or modify the USITC's recommendations, the AD and CVD statutes provide for virtually automatic imposition of import restrictions.

The Trade Agreements Act of 1979 amended the AD and CVD statutes to provide the executive branch with a limited flexibility. Under this authority, the ITA may reach agreements that resolve subsidy or dumping disputes "out of court" before CVD or AD duties are levied. Congress intended that this authority be used sparingly, and established criteria to assure that the petitioner was satisfied and/or that the unfair trade practices or their injurious effects were nullified.

If the petitioner is satisfied by the agreement, it may withdraw the petition. Once a petition is withdrawn, the case will be terminated. If the petitioner will not withdraw, the ITA can suspend but not terminate the investigation. No suspension agreement can be accepted unless the ITA is satisfied that suspension is in the public interest, that the agreement could be monitored, and that the agreement precludes import surges during the period necessary for its full implementation.

There are two basic types of agreement. In the first instance, the foreign government (or exporters that account for substantially all the unfairly traded products) will agree to cease exports within six months of the agreement, or to take steps to eliminate or offset the subsidy completely, or to revise its pricing to eliminate sales at less than fair value. The second type of agreement focuses on eliminating the injurious effect of these imports on U.S. producers. These agreements can only be entered into if the ITA determines that extraordinary conditions exist (meaning that suspension would be more beneficial to the domestic industry than the continuation of the investigation) and that the investigation is complex. Agreements eliminating the injurious effect of these imports must involve price undertakings that either offset at least 85 percent of the net subsidy or eliminate 85 percent of the dumping margin uncovered in the investigation. The agreement must also prevent the undercutting or suppression of U.S. price levels. In subsidy cases, the ITA can enter into voluntary export-restraint agreements with the foreign government to offset the injurious effect.

The ITA cannot suspend an investigation until after it has reached a preliminary determination that the product in question is subsidized or dumped. If the petitioner accepts the decision, the proceedings are suspended, liquidation continues, and no security or deposit is required on the estimated duties. If a suspended proceeding is later resumed, it is taken up at the point of suspension.

Petitioners can request the USITC to determine whether the agreement has eliminated the material injury caused by the unfairly traded product. If the USITC finds that the agreement does not eliminate the injurious effects, then the suspension agreement is terminated and the proceedings recommence.

The legislative history of the settlement and suspension authorities reveals that Congress intended for such agreements to be the exception rather than the rule, and until recently the ITA has been cautious in its use of this authority.[20] A great many settlement agreements were reached in 1982, when trade-remedy petitions from the U.S. steel industry inundated the ITA. That year, the ITA reached agreements with the European Community that led to the withdrawal of forty-four petitions submitted by fifteen domestic steel producers. Similar procedures were followed in the implementation of President Reagan's national steel program, in which several petitions were withdrawn in early 1985 (see chapter 7).

Public Interest Test

Before the TTA, there was no public interest test required for terminations, and only a vaguely defined test for suspension agreements which eliminated the injurious effect. The TTA establishes new procedures and considerations for certain CVD and AD terminations, and for suspensions in some CVD cases. The TTA provides criteria for an explicit public interest test for suspensions of CVD investigations based on quantitative restrictions, and extends the same requirements to terminations based on quantitative agreements. If the criteria are not met, the ITA may not suspend or terminate the case, and the proceedings must continue.

The TTA provides that the ITA must take into account whether, based upon consumer prices and the availability of supplies, the agreement would have a greater adverse impact on U.S. consumers than would the imposition of countervailing duties. The ITA must also consider the relative impact on the international economic interests of the United States and the relative impact on the competitiveness of the domestic industry producing the like merchandise. The act also provides that in reaching this determination, the department must consult with nonparticipating parties, including potentially affected consuming industries as well as producers and workers in the domestic industry manufacturing the like merchandise. The producers and workers that are consulted need not be parties to the investigation.

The provision was included out of concern that some foreign and domestic industries would prefer quotas to the elimination of the unfair trade practices, because quotas allow the two parties to benefit from the high cost of artificially scarce goods (quota rents) without actually eliminating the subsidy or the dumping margin. The Congress prefers that unfair trade practices be eliminated entirely or, failing that, that they be offset by appropriate duties. The public interest test and the consultations with nonparticipating interested parties were written into the law so that it would be more difficult to use the CVD provisions as an indirect means to achieve quotas.

It is notable that the Reagan administration opposed this amendment. In its view, the explicit public interest test was unnecessary, as the ITA already took the interests of consumers and others to heart in deciding whether suspension or termination agreements are an acceptable alternative to CVD or ADs. Moreover, the "greater adverse impact" provision was said to be an unworkable standard that would only serve to limit executive discretion.[21]

As of this writing, the public interest test has not had any discernible impact. It was applied in only a *pro forma* manner when several steel petitions were withdrawn in early 1985, based on quantitative restrictions.

Consultations to Eliminate Unfair Trade Practices

The act amends the procedures that are followed after a CVD suspension agreement involving quantitative restrictions is in effect. Suspension agreements must be reviewed annually by the ITA, and by the USITC whenever the commission receives information showing that circumstances warrant a review. If the USITC determines in its review that the suspension agreement no longer eliminates the injurious effect of the imports, then the ITA and the USITC renew their investigations at the point where they were frozen.

There was no provision prior to the TTA that required the executive to seek the elimination of the subsidy while the agreement was in effect, or to impose offsetting duties upon its expiration. Section 614 directs the president "within 90 days after the ITA accepts a quantitative restriction agreement . . . [to] enter into consultations with the government that is party to the agreement" in order to eliminate the subsidy completely, or reduce the new subsidy to a level that completely eliminates the injurious effect. This amendment further provides that the president may require the ITA to modify an agreement that establishes quantitative restrictions. Before the expiration of the agreement, the ITA initiates a proceeding to determine the existence and amount of any remaining subsidy. If the ITA reaches a positive determination, then the USITC determines whether imports would cause or threaten material injury upon the termination of the agreement. The commission may then determine whether a CVD should be imposed.

This provision could be rather unsettling for foreign exporters. It puts the foreign supplier under a double jeopardy of negotiated settlements, first with the suspension agreement and later with the postagreement consultations. The provision also subjects them to immediate countervailing action upon the expiration of the agreement. It reflects congressional concern that the principal objective of the statute—the elimination or offset of unfair trade practices—may be flouted.

Although the amendment might seem to expand the negotiating powers of the executive branch, the Reagan administration opposed it. The administration argued that it "would unnecessarily bring the President into the process of negotiating and administering suspension agreements."[22]

Termination of Self-Initiated CVD Investigations

Prior to the TTA, the ITA could terminate AD investigations that it had self-initiated, but the law made no such provision for CVD cases. This oversight is corrected by Section 604 of the TTA, which states that the ITA has an unconditional right to terminate these investigations on its own motion.

Assessment and Payment of Duties

After a final affirmative USITC finding, the ITA must issue a final CVD or AD order that specifies the duty that it has determined to be necessary in order to offset the unfair trade practices. The Customs Service is directed to assess duties on merchandise subject to the suspension of liquidation and to require deposits of the estimated CVD or AD duty for the next twelve-month period. This procedure continues annually until the AD or CVD order is revoked. Security may be posted in lieu of the actual deposit of estimated duty payments for up to ninety days if the ITA believes that it can complete a review of the dumping margin and establish a new final rate within that time. If the final duty for the period is less than the provisional rate, the difference will be refunded. If the final duty exceeds the provisional rate, no additional payment is due from the importer.

Waiver of Deposits on Estimated Duties. Prior to the TTA, bonds or other security could be posted on estimated AD duties during the period between a preliminary affirmative determination and the final determination. This was a less onerous alternative than posting actual deposits. The new legislation restricts this waiver to entries that are entered and resold to unrelated purchasers.

Prior Deposits for CVDs. Section 738 of the Tariff Act of 1930 requires that duties be deposited with the Customs Service prior to entries or removal from warehouse of goods that are subject to an AD order. There was previously no parallel requirement for CVD cases on the books, but the ITA applied one on its own authority. The act codifies this practice.

Drawback of CVDs. A drawback program in U.S. trade law allows exporters who use imported inputs in their products to receive refunds for the import duties they paid on imported inputs if these inputs are used to produce exported products. The drawback provision currently treats ADs as import duties for purposes of the program. Section 779 of the TTA provides that CVDs may also be drawn back by exporters.

Interest Rates. The act changes the rate of interest that may be assessed or reimbursed for under- or overpayment. The rate is changed from "8 percent or the rate in effect when duties were determined, whichever is higher" to the rate established under the Internal Revenue Code. The legislation also clarifies that the date on which interest becomes payable is the date of publication of a CVD or AD order, or of an AD finding, and not the date of publication of a USITC determination.

Country-wide Assessment of CVDs. Section 607 of the TTA establishes a "presumption" of country-wide CVD rates to be assessed on all suppliers from a country, rather than applying distinct CVDs to individual companies. Differing CVDs may still be applied if the ITA determines that there is a significant difference in benefits received by companies, or if a state-owned enterprise is involved. The legislative intent of this provision is to decrease the administrative burden that company-specific rates impose. One consequence of the law, however, may be the blurring of distinctions between producers. It could lead to some firms paying duties that are disproportionate to the subsidies they received, while some subsidized exporters might avoid duties, or be required to pay duties that are lower than those which might be established under company-specific rates.

Judicial Review

The Court of International Trade (known before 1980 as the Customs Court) has jurisdiction over the trade-remedy laws, with appellate authority resting with the Court of Appeals for the Federal Circuit. Prior to the TTA, these courts could review preliminary negative decisions to find whether the determination was "arbitrary, capricious, an abuse of discretion, or otherwise not in accordance with the law." This was a limited scope for review, and discriminated against respondents by applying to negative decisions that only the petitioners would wish to appeal. Final determinations could be reviewed on much broader grounds to determine if they are "unsupported by substantial evidence on the record, or otherwise not in accordance with the law" and could be requested by petitioner or respondent.

Elimination of Interlocutory Appeals. Section 623 of the act eliminates all judicial reviews prior to the final determination stage. The principal reason behind this change is the congressional concern over frequent and costly appeals to the CIT. Interlocutory appeals added an additional complication to the proceedings and contributed to the great expense associated with trade-remedy laws.

Appeals of Negative Decisions. The same section clarifies the circumstances under which appeals may be made, particularly in the case of negative sections of affirmative decisions. If a final affirmative decision specifically excludes any company or product from its scope, then the petitioners may treat this portion of the decision as a negative finding for purposes of judicial appeal. The act further states that final affirmative determinations by the ITA may be contested if the USITC subsequently issues a negative injury determination that is predicated on the small size of the dumping margin or the net subsidy. Margins analysis, however, is generally not critical in the USITC's deliberations.

Administrative Review and Revocation

The law mandates annual reviews of CVD and AD orders as well as suspension agreements. During these reviews, the ITA is to determine the current status of the subsidy or dumping practice which gave rise to the order. If a suspension agreement is in effect, then the ITA must determine whether the foreign supplier is still in compliance with its terms. If circumstances warrant, the ITA may renew a suspended investigation or adjust the duty.

The ITA or USITC can institute a review of the final determinations themselves if there is evidence of changed circumstances. AD orders can be revoked or suspended investigations can be terminated if the ITA determines that the merchandise in question has not been sold at less than fair value for the preceding two years or that the merchandise has not been shipped for four years. CVD orders can be revoked or suspended investigations can be terminated if the subsidy program has been abolished for the imports in question for three consecutive years and the subsidy program is not likely to be reinstated.

Alternatively, revocation or termination can take place if the foreign producers have not applied for or received a net subsidy for at least five years, and are not likely to apply for or benefit from such a subsidy. Revocation or termination will also take place if the USITC determines that material injury would not result from such action.

Burden of Persuasion. The TTA states that "the party seeking revocation of an antidumping order shall have the burden of persuasion with respect to whether there are changed circumstances sufficient to warrant revocation of an antidumping order." This provision was added in response to the 1983 decision of the Court of International Trade in the case of *Matsushita* v. *United States,* where the court (in the view of the House–Senate conferees) "incorrectly place[d] the burden of persuasion on the domestic industry."[23]

Annual Reviews Only on Request. The new legislation provides that annual reviews need only be held upon request. This simplifies the operation of the system and benefits the administering agencies, the petitioners, and respondents. None of them need to bear the burden of annual reviews if these are not necessary, but either the petitioner or the foreign supplier may request such a review.

The act further specifies that the ITA need only verify information that is used in the review of a CVD or AD order if the information was not verified in either of the two previous reviews, and the petitioner requests verification. This will reduce the administrative burden imposed by mandatory verification.

Export Taxes Not a Sufficient Cause for Revocation. Section 611 of the TTA provides that the USITC may not revoke a CVD order or terminate a suspended investigation solely on the basis of any export taxes, duties, or charges that are levied on products exported to the United States in order to offset the effect of subsidies. This amendment reflects congressional concern over allegations that some countries were not observing their obligations to offset export subsidies. It mirrors a similar provision in the TTA that disallows negative determinations based on offsets. Export taxes can be used as a basis for the suspension of investigations, but not as the basis for negative determinations or the termination of investigations.

Revocations Based on Lack of Interest. Orders may be revoked or suspended investigations may be terminated at any time, if the ITA concludes that no interest is shown in the continuation of an order. This determination will be made on the basis of available information, including an affirmative statement of no interest from the petitioner. This change emanates from a comment in the conference report interpreting section 611 of the TTA to mean that ITA "should be able to revoke antidumping or countervailing duties that are no longer of interest.[24] This is the first time that the ITA has issued regulations allowing it to revoke an existing order or terminate a proceeding despite existing determinations of unfair trade practices and material injury. Not only can this provision reduce the ITA's workload, it may also open the possibilities for negotiations in which petitioners will request revocation.

The possible implications of this provision were evident during the negotiation of voluntary export restraints on steel, when the Department of Commerce arranged for the revocation of CVD and AD orders in exchange for the conclusion of voluntary restraint agreements (see chapter 7). In one case involving oil country tubular goods (OCTG), the company that had originally lodged the petition did not want to withdraw, although the majority of the domestic U.S. petitioners supported withdrawal as a precondition for a more comprehensive market restriction. The reluctance of this single company to withdraw threatened to spoil agreements that had been reached with Brazil, Mexico, and Spain, all of which were promised that the AD and CVD cases would be terminated. The petitioner finally recanted when faced with the reported possibility that the Department of Commerce would rule that the expressed desire of the majority of domestic petitioners was sufficient cause to terminate the case. The precedential value of this case may be weak, given the fact that the Department of Commerce did not actually terminate the case against the will of the petitioner, but it does suggest the potential for an activist ITA posture in possible future negotiations.

Similarly, if no requests are made to review an outstanding CVD or AD order for a five-year period, the ITA may revoke an order or terminate a suspended investigation.

Violation of Suspension Agreements. The Secretary of Commerce is required to inform the Customs Service of any suspected violations of suspension agreements. If the violation is deemed to be intentional, Customs may confiscate the merchandise. This reflects congressional concern over alleged failure of some countries to honor commitments made with the United States.

Notes

1. The so-called "seven dwarfs" are El Salvador, Honduras, Liberia, Nepal, North Yemen, Paraguay, and Venezuela.

2. The natural resources subsidization proposal would have extended the definition of subsidies to cover domestic prices for natural resource inputs that are lower than export sales prices for the same inputs. The inputs that would be affected by this proposal include natural gas, petroleum, and timber, while the end products cover a potentially vast range of goods. This proposal would contravene the established rule that government programs or subsidies that are generally available throughout the economy are not subject to countervailing action. The Reagan administration argued that this would be in clear violation of the GATT. The issue reemerged in the 99th Congress.

3. The downstream dumping provision would have expanded the coverage of the antidumping statute by directing the ITA to examine the prices of inputs used in imported products. It would have defined an end product to have been dumped if one of its pricipal components was sold to the producer at less than fair value. For example, if Producer A sold valves to an unrelated party (Producer B) at less than their fair market price, and Producer B used these valves to make engines, then Producer B's engines sold in the United States could be considered dumped—even if the price was at or above the fair market price. A very similar proposal converning so-called "diversionary dumping" was later made in the 99th Congress (see chapter 8).

4. Communist countries, known in trade policy jargon as *nonmarket economies* (NMEs) or *state-controlled economies* (SCEs), are subject to special rules in U.S. trade-remedy laws. Communist countries are only accorded most-favored-nation treatment if they meet the emigration and other requirements set by the Jackson–Vanik amendment to the Trade Act of 1974; countries that do not fulfill these conditions (including the Soviet Union) are subject to the high column 2 duty rates of the Tariff Schedules, which have changed little since they were set by the Smoot–Hawley Tariff Act of 1930. It is questionable whether the nonmarket economies are subject to the U.S. antisubsidy laws. The ITA decided in 1984 that subsidies were a meaningless concept in economies that have no market mechanism. The Court of International Trade (CIT) reversed this decision in a 1985 ruling, and the ITA subsequently appealed the CIT's ruling. Communist countries are the subject of section 406 of the Trade Act of 1974, a trade-remedy law intended to halt the disruptive imports from nonmarket countries. Exports to these countries are controlled by the Export Administration Act of 1979 (as amended in 1985).

The nonmarket economy dumping proposal floated in the 98th Congress would have subjected most communist countries to stricter application of the antidumping laws by denying the injury test to NMEs that are not members of the GATT. The amendment would also alter the price comparison, so that the exports in question would in the first instance be compared against an average price of market economy exports to the United States. Because this average is likely in most cases to be higher than the price charged by the NMEs, this provision would increase the probability of dumping findings. The target countries included the USSR, East Germany, Bulgaria, and the People's Republic of China (P.R.C.). The administration's opposition was largely due to concern over the measure's implications for U.S.-P.R.C. trade relations.

5. Baldrige and Brock expressed the administration's position on trade-remedy reform in a joint letter sent on April 3, 1984 to House Ways and Means Committee Chairman Dan Rostenkowski. This letter was accompanied by several detailed position papers on the major and minor amendments to the trade statutes that were then under consideration. The letter and the position papers were printed as pp. 166–203 in U.S. Senate, Committee on Finance, *Problems of Access by Small Businesses to Trade Remedies.* 98th Congress, 2d session, Senate Hearing Print 98-1043 (April 6, 1984).

6. The Court of International Trade issued a series of rulings in mid-1985 that reversed several USITC preliminary negative determinations. The CIT argued that the commission had applied an unnecessarily strict standard at an early stage of the proceedings. As of this writing, it is unclear to what extent the CIT decisions will lead commissioners to lower their threshold of injury in this phase of their trade-remedy investigations.

7. U.S. International Trade Commission, *Certain Table Wine from France and Italy.* USITC Publication 1502 (March 1984).

8. U.S. International Trade Commission, *Certain Table Wine from the Federal Republic of Germany, France, and Italy.* USITC Publication 1771 (October 1985).

9. See Senate Hearing Print 98–1043 (cited in note 6), *passim.*

10. The TTA actually refers to a Trade Remedy Assistance *Office,* but the commission apparently preferred the title *Center.*

11. U.S. International Trade Commission, *Certain Rail Passenger Cars and Parts Thereof from Canada.* USITC Publication 1277 (August 1982).

12. See M. Stuart Madden, "The Threat of Material Injury Standard in Countervailing Duty Enforcement," *Law and Policy in International Business* 16, no. 2 (1984): 373–416.

13. U.S. International Trade Commission, *Certain Oil Country Tubular Goods from Brazil, Korea and Spain.* USITC Publication 1633 (January 1985).

14. See Gary C. Hufbauer and Joanna Shelton Erb, *Subsidies in International Trade* (Washington, D.C.: Institute for International Economics, 1984), pp. 93–95.

15. See the ITA notice in the *Federal Register* 50, no. 111 (June 10, 1985): 24270–76.

16. See the ITA notice in the *Federal Register* 50, no. 165 (August 26, 1985): 34525–37.

17. For discussions of the industrial targeting issue, as well as case studies, see the three-volume study of the U.S. International Trade Commission entitled *Foreign Industrial Targeting and Its Effects on U.S. Industries.* Phase I of the study deals with Japan, and was issued in October 1983 as USITC publication 1437. Phase II, which concentrates on the European Community and its member states, was issued as Publication 1517 in April 1984. Phase III covers Brazil, Canada, South Korea, Mexico, and Taiwan, and was issued as Publication 1632 in January 1985. See also the GAO, Department of Labor, and USTR studies cited in notes 18 and 19.

For the views of U.S. industry and labor groups that oppose foreign targeting practices, see Labor–Industry Coalition for International Trade (LICIT), *International Trade, Industrial Policies, and the Future of American Industry* (Washington, D.C.: LICIT, April 1983). See also President's Export Council, *Industrial Targeting: Foreign Industrial Targeting Practices and Possible U.S. Responses* (Washington, D.C.: U.S. Department of Commerce, December 1984).

18. General Accounting Office, *Foreign Industrial Targeting—U.S. Trade Law Remedies.* GAO/NSIAD-85-77 (May 23, 1985), p. iv. See also U.S. Department of Labor, "Trade and Employment Effects of Foreign Industrial Targeting: Results of Three Case Studies" (mimeo, July 1985).

19. U.S. Trade Representative, "Report on Foreign Industrial Targeting" (mimeo, July 1985), p. 31.

20. For an excellent discussion of ITA policy and other issues surrounding the use of such agreements, see Alan F. Holmer and Judith H. Bello, "Suspension and Settlement Agreements in Unfair Trade Cases," *The International Lawyer* 18, no. 3 (Summer 1984): 683–97.

21. Baldrige and Brock, *op. cit.,* p. 184.

22. *Ibid.*

23. U.S. House of Representatives, *Trade and Tariff Act of 1984 Conference Report.* 98th Congress, 2d session, report 98–1156 (October 5, 1984), p. 182.

24. *Ibid.,* p. 181.

Part III
Other Provisions
of the TTA

7
Steel Import Relief and Other Specific Product Measures

The Steel Import Stabilization Act of 1984

The Steel Import Stabilization Act of 1984 (title VIII of the TTA) provides the executive branch with the authority to enforce the voluntary steel export restraints negotiated with foreign governments. Title VIII is the latest in a long series of special measures intended to bolster the ailing U.S. steel industry.

History of Protection for the U.S. Steel Industry

The U.S. carbon steel industry was the unchallenged world leader following the Second World War, but the refurbished plants of Europe and Japan slowly began to overtake their American competitors. Several of the developing countries later joined the ranks of world class steel producers, and compounded the difficulties faced by the U.S. mills. Imports had accounted for only 1.4 percent of domestic consumption in 1950, but grew to 4.8 percent in 1960, 13.8 percent in 1970, and 20.6 percent in 1983. U.S. steel imports exceeded exports for the first time in 1959.[1] With foreign producers capturing an ever larger share of the market, U.S. steel producers gradually abandoned their earlier commitment to liberal trade.

Over the past three decades, the U.S. steel industry has resorted to almost every conceivable form of trade remedy and import relief program, in an effort to stave off growing foreign competition. The industry filed nearly three hundred antidumping petitions from 1961 to 1967, but only eight of these were ultimately decided in their favor. As an alternative to the trade-remedy statutes, the industry enlisted the government's aid in negotiating voluntary restraint agreements (VRAs) on the part of Europe and Japan. Grey-area measures such as VRAs are an atypical departure from the GATT in that they do not apply equally to imports from all sources and do not require compensation because they are putatively voluntary. The European and Japanese VRAs remained in place from 1968 through 1974.

Two years after the VRAs expired, the specialty steel producers (a small sector of the steel industry) petitioned for relief under the escape clause. The relief was granted in the form of a three-year quota on their products, which was eventually extended until 1980. In 1978, the Carter administration instituted a new relief program with an innovative trigger price mechanism (TPM) for imported steel. The TPM established a trigger based on the price levels of Japanese producers, who were considered to be the most efficient in the world. Any imports that entered below the specified price or any import surges from a particular country might trigger the self-initiation of antidumping proceedings by the U.S. government. The principle behind this mechanism was that foreign producers could not undersell the Japanese without dumping. With some interruption during 1980, the TPM remained in place until January 1982.

The specialty steel producers filed a series of section 301 petitions with the Office of the U.S. Trade Representative in 1981, alleging that several European producers violated U.S. rights by subsidizing their steel exports. President Reagan responded the next year by requesting that the U.S. International Trade Commission initiate an escape-clause investigation of five specialty steel products. The escape-clause proceedings led to an affirmative USITC decision, followed by the 1983 imposition of quotas on some products, tariffs on others, and the negotiation of orderly marketing agreements (OMAs) with seven foreign suppliers. Like VRAs, OMAs are grey-area measures that do not require compensation for the affected trading partner.

An unprecedented flurry of activity in the USITC and International Trade Administration of the Department of Commerce occurred in 1982, when the U.S. steel industry swamped the agencies with more than two hundred antidumping and antisubsidy petitions. In contrast to the low success rate for the petitions filed from 1961 to 1967, nearly one in four of the cases that were completed resulted in AD or CVD orders against foreign suppliers. In order to avoid the likely imposition of duties on their own products, the European Community negotiated with the United States an Arrangement Concerning Trade in Certain Steel Products and a complementary Arrangement on Pipe and Tube Products. In exchange for the EC's promise to limit its exports to specified market shares for various steel products and to consult on problems caused in related products, the U.S. industry withdrew its petitions against the EC, while the ITA terminated the investigation.

The 1984 Maneuvers

The steel industry's campaign for import protection culminated in a three-pronged assault in 1984. The industry simultaneously urged that the Congress enact a Fair Trade in Steel Act of 1984 (H.R. 5081), and filed an escape clause with the USITC on carbon steel products. The steel bill and the relief requested under the escape clause would both establish an import quota of 15 percent.

According to Donald Trautlein, chief executive officer of the Bethlehem Steel Corporation, "The problem is simply too important to rely entirely on either process."[2] As added insurance, the industry filed many antidumping and countervailing duty petitions. Nearly all significant suppliers were vulnerable to these petitions, the only notable exceptions being Japan and South Korea.

The industry hoped to capitalize on the political pressures of an election year. The submission of the escape-clause petition was timed so that, should the commission recommend that import relief be granted, the president would be forced to act on the USITC recommendations during the height of the presidential campaign. The industry also hoped that the Congress would feel compelled to vote for import relief as the November elections drew nearer.

The Reagan administration voiced its strong opposition to the industry's initiatives. Ambassador William Brock, the U.S. Trade Representative, argued that the proposed quotas would undermine U.S. competitiveness in the industries that depend on steel as a raw material, and would lead U.S. trading partners to retaliate by closing their markets to U.S. exports. He urged that "painful, yet essential cost reductions must continue if this industry is going to survive and prosper."[3]

The steel quota legislation appeared to enjoy widespread support in the House, although passage in the Senate was uncertain. Capitol Hill postponed action on the legislation in order to pressure the Reagan administration into resolving the escape-clause case in favor of the domestic industry.

On June 12, the USITC reached affirmative injury determinations on most of the products that were subject to investigation. Among the key factors that the commissioners cited in reaching this determination were the decline of steel mill shipments to a twenty-year low in 1982, a capacity utilization rate of just 56.2 percent in 1983, and a 41-percent drop in employment between 1979 and 1983. Two weeks later, the commission recommended to the president that a tariff-rate quota be imposed on semifinished steel; that quotas be placed on imports of plates, sheets, strip, structurals, and wire; and that duties be increased on wire products. The USITC plan would last for five years. Two of the commissioners further recommended that the relief plan be conditioned on the presentation of adjustment plans by the steel industry.[4]

The President's Steel Plan

The U.S. steel industry had banked on the hope that the presidential election would make import relief irresistible for President Reagan, but reelection seemed to be a near certainty by the late summer of 1984. The political arguments in favor of protectionism were further weakened during the Democratic primaries, when Senator Gary Hart's liberal trade views appeared to win him more converts than did Walter Mondale's reputed predeliction for market restrictions.

Although the political imperative for import relief had faded, the White House decided that a compromise was necessary to placate the steel industry and forestall passage of more stringent steel quota legislation. The White House announced on September 18, 1984 that import relief under the escape clause was not in the national economic interest, but the administration developed its own relief plan outside of the escape clause. The central element of the president's plan was to continue and tighten the existing voluntary restraint agreements with the EC and other producers, and to negotiate new VRAs with the "uncontrolled" suppliers. The restraints would cover all products, not just those which the USITC had found to be causing or threatening injury. The ultimate goal was to keep import penetration down to a target of 18.5 percent of domestic consumption for finished steel, or approximately 20.2 percent if semifabricated steel was included in the calculation. Other elements of the White House plan included vigorous prosecution of alleged unfair trade practices by foreign producers as well as the negotiation of new controls on import surges from some foreign suppliers.

The White House plan technically constituted a rejection of import relief under the escape clause and was predicated on voluntary agreements. This had two important consequences. First, it meant that the United States would not be automatically bound to offer compensation to its trading partners for any market restrictions it set in place. Second, by going outside of the procedures laid out in the escape clause, the president had no inherent authority to enforce his plan. This made it necessary to request that the Congress grant the U.S. Customs Service the power to police the import controls at the border. Any steel shipments made from countries with which the United States negotiated a VRA would need licenses in order to enter the U.S. market.

Once the president's plan was announced, the Congress took the initiative. House Ways and Means Committee Chairman Dan Rostenkowski (Dem.-Ill.) developed a proposal that he modeled on presidential candidate Walter Mondale's program for the steel industry. The Rostenkowski legislation would have required the president to enforce the quantitative limits on steel imports that he pledged to negotiate, but also established the sense of the Congress that the target for import penetration should be set at 17 rather than 20.2 percent. The bill would further require that steel producers commit their net cash flow to modernization programs, except for 1 percent set aside for worker retraining.

Title VIII of the TTA

The House–Senate conference committee on the Trade and Tariff Act crafted a compromise between the president's plan and Chairman Rostenkowski's bill. In place of the president's import penetration goal of 20.2 percent and the Mondale/Rostenkowski figure of 17 percent, the TTA specifies that it is the sense of the Congress that the foreign share of the domestic market be in the range of 17 to 20.2 percent (depending on whether semifinished steel is counted) "subject to such modifications that changes in market conditions and the composition of the steel industry may require." Like other sense of the Congress resolutions, these terms are not binding on the executive branch.

Title VIII of the TTA provides the executive branch with the five-year enforcement authority needed to restrict steel imports from those countries that agree to voluntary restraints, but makes continued relief conditional upon the cooperation of the domestic steel producers. The president must certify annually to the Congress that the major steel companies (that is, those whose 1983 raw steel production exceeded 1.5 million net tons) have "committed substantially all of their net cash flow from steel product operations" to reinvestment and modernization, "taken sufficient action to maintain their international competitiveness," and committed "not less than 1 percent of net cash flow to the retraining of workers." The last requirement can be waived if the president finds that unusual circumstances exist in a company. The modernization provisions are complemented by section 807 of the TTA, which instructs the Secretaries of Labor and Commerce to prepare a plan to assist displaced steel workers in relocation and retraining. The departments were given six months to prepare this plan.

These provisions set a significant precedent. To the chagrin of the Reagan administration, they represent a cautious step toward a national industrial policy. The White House remains oppposed to any policies that entail government involvement in economic planning, but it was unable to defeat this Democratic initiative.

Negotiation of the VRAs

The outstanding orders and pending investigations proved helpful to the U.S. steel negotiators. By offering to arrange for the withdrawal of petitions by the U.S. industry, they were able to entice suppliers to agree to limit their exports voluntarily. Upon withdrawal of a petition, the Commerce Department would then terminate the case. When AD or CVD orders were already in place, the U.S. industry could show its "lack of interest" in the continuation of the order.[5] If a voluntary accord were violated, the Department of Commerce would process the case on an expedited basis.

As of November 1985, the United States had negotiated VRAs with 15 countries. Canada is the only major steel supplier that is not subject to a restraint agreement, although the Reagan administration has come under heavy pressure from the domestic industry to reach an accord with Canada. The VRAs work by limiting the exporting nation to a designated share of the U.S. market in individual categories of steel products, with a certain degree of flexibility for shifting shares among a country's categories (that is, shipping more of one product in exchange for less of another). The market shares agreed to in the

VRAs represent a rollback from the record import penetration levels of 1984 (see table 7-1).

The negotiations were comparatively more damaging for developing countries than they were for established suppliers in the industrialized nations. The developed countries have generally held stable shares of the U.S. steel market, while the third world has experienced (and probably would have continued to experience) rapid growth in steel shipments to the United States. Freezing market shares is obviously more consequential for countries that would otherwise enjoy a growing export market.

Negotiations with the European Community proved to be particularly difficult and prolonged. The initial agreement did not specify limits on pipe and tube exports—products that are of particular concern to the U.S. industry—and ran for a short period of time. Title VIII of the TTA provided the president with the authority to enforce the 1982 Arrangement on Pipe and Tube Products, even though the original arrangement had no agreed enforcement mechanism, and the Reagan administration had specifically requested that no such provision be included in the TTA. The administration overcame its earlier qualms, and used this authority to embargo imports of EC steel pipes and tubes during December 1984. The embargo was lifted after the two sides negotiated a new agreement in January 1985, but the United States came close to closing the market for EC steel twice in 1985. As of this writing, a new U.S.–EC steel agreement has been reached, but an accord on EC shipments of semifinished steel is still elusive.

Table 7-1
Share of Apparent U.S. Consumption of Carbon Steel Imports, 1984, and Voluntary Restraint Agreement Limits
(in percentages)

	1984 Market Share	VRA Limit
European Community	5.90	5.50
Japan	7.05	5.80
South Korea	2.48	1.90
Brazil	1.42	0.80
Spain	1.45	0.67
Mexico	0.83	0.36
Australia	0.20	0.18
South Africa	0.59	0.42
Finland	0.30	0.22
Venezuela	0.51	0.20
Poland	0.14	0.10
Romania	0.28	0.16
Hungary	0.04	0.04
Czechoslovakia	0.07	0.04
East Germany	0.29	0.12

Source: Press accounts and unpublished U.S. government data.

Japan and South Korea were in a unique position. Both are efficient producers that do not rely on unfair trade practices, and therefore were comparatively
immune to pressure via trade-remedy petitions. The two countries were never-
theless willing to voluntarily limit their exports, but objected to the specific
terms proposed by the U.S. negotiators. Compromise solutions were reached
only after the USTR drew up a list of complaints against Korea and threatened to
self-initiate investigations under the section 301 presidential retaliation authority (see chapter 2), and the congressional steel caucus proposed legislation that
would have unilaterally restricted steel imports from Japan. The threat of these
actions brought both countries to reach export restraint agreements with the
United States.

Developments since the Steel Negotiations

As of November 1985, the effectiveness of the president's steel program was still
in doubt. Steel imports amounted to 25.62 percent of apparent domestic
consumption in the first 8 months of 1985, compared with 26.65 percent for all
of 1984.[6] With this modest reduction in import penetration, the administration
goal of keeping imports down to 18.5–20.2 percent of domestic consumption
seemed well out of reach. Some observers felt that the total figures for 1985
would show a lower penetration level, as some of the countries subject to VRAs
filled up their quotas early in the year. An analysis by the Congressional
Research Service (CRS) was less sanguine. The CRS concluded on the basis of
the 15 VRAs negotiated thus far that imports from other nations would have to
be trimmed by 32 percent if the administration's goal were to be reached.[7] The
analysis projected an overall import penetration level of 22.6 percent for the
duration of the steel restraint program (that is, through 1989).

Far from decreasing, shipments from unrestrained nations appear to have
increased rapidly. The limitations placed on the major suppliers created opportunities for other producers. In some cases, the steel exports have originated in
countries with no known domestic production, thus raising the question of
fraudulent invoicing or transshipments designed to thwart the VRAs.[8] The U.S.
producers have also expressed concern over the apparent foreign practice of
shifting production and exports from low- to high-value steel products, in order
to get the most out of their quotas.

The TTA warned that if the steel policy "does not produce satisfactory
results within a reasonable period of time," then the Congress "will consider
taking such legislative actions concerning steel and iron ore products as may be
necessary or appropriate to stabilize conditions in the domestic market for such
products." Although dissatisfaction with the initial results of the program had
led some congressmen to introduce new steel legislation in the 99th Congress—
with the proposals ranging from new enforcement powers for the U.S. Customs
Service to unilateral quotas for unrestrained suppliers—the prospects for new
legislation looked unlikely in late 1985.

Marking Requirements

The TTA creates new regulations for country-of-origin marking for steel pipes and tubes, as well as for manhole covers and compressed gas cylinders. These products must be "marked with the English name of the country of origin by means of die stamping, cast-in-mold lettering, etching, or engraving." Importers and producers of foreign steel have complained that this measure constitutes a nontariff barrier and that markings of this sort could harm the integrity of the steel. There is also some concern that the requirements could be applied to very small piping that cannot be subjected to this type of marking.

In response to these criticisms, complete implementation of the provision was temporarily postponed. Remedial legislation may be enacted in the 99th Congress.

Other Specific Product Measures

Sense of the Congress Resolutions

The relationship between the executive and legislative branches in trade policy is delicate. The Congress naturally wishes to exercise some influence in the direction of U.S. trade policy, but recognizes that the executive branch needs to be flexible in its dealings with foreign governments. One means for the Congress to express its desires without hamstringing the executive branch is to enact resolutions that state the sense of the Congress. These resolutions are not binding upon the executive branch, nor do they provide new negotiating authority to achieve the objectives they present. Their value lies in the clear signals they send to the executive branch as well as to the foreign governments, with both groups being put on notice that an issue is of significant concern to Capitol Hill. Among the sense of the Congress resolutions in the TTA are provisions calling for the president to oppose European proposals to increase protective barriers to U.S. agricultural exports, pursue discussions with the Canadian government to resolve a dispute over Canadian price supports for hogs and pork products, negotiate voluntary production-restraint agreements with foreign copper producers, and take action against Japan if the Japanese Diet approves legislation limiting copyright protection for computer software.

Tariff Changes and Reclassifications

Titles I and II of the TTA make temporary and permanent changes in the tariff rates and classifications of dozens of items in the Tariff Schedules of the United States (TSUS). The majority of these provisions are liberalizing measures that temporarily reduce or suspend duties. Some of the more important changes reclassify the tariff nomenclature of several telecommunications products, grant the president power to implement tariff reductions negotiated in the Agreement on Trade in Civil Aircraft, and effectively raise the tariff on frozen concentrated orange juice.

Customs Measures

The Trade and Tariff Act of 1984 authorizes the FY1985 budget for the U.S. Customs Service and also addresses the powers, policies, and procedures of that agency. The majority of these measures consist of minor adjustments in existing laws or special grants of dispensation to certain nonprofit importers, but some provisions of the new legislation make important changes in particular areas. These include a provision that denies the tariff advantages of free trade zones to bicycles manufactured from otherwise dutiable parts, a prohibition on state and local taxation of property in free trade zones, redefinition of certain rules in the duty-drawback program, an improvement in Puerto Rico's status in the Caribbean Basin Initiative, and a unique measure stating that articles returned from space will not be considered to have been imported (and therefore not subject to entry procedures and import charges) under certain circumstances.

The old law regulating customhouse brokers dates from 1910, and was incorporated in the Tariff Act of 1930 with virtually no changes. The Customs Brokers Act of 1984 (section 212 of the TTA) is the first substantial reform of the legislation in nearly seventy-five years. Although a few of the provisions will have a major impact on the profession, most of them bring the legislation up to date with existing practices. The thrust of the reform is to allow the brokers greater control over their own activities. The legislation defines the term *customs business* and restricts the scope of Customs Service power over customs brokers to customs business. It also specifies that only licensed brokers may conduct customs business for third parties, sets forth licensing and permit procedures, establishes a duty for customs brokers to exercise responsibility and control over their customs business, and formulates disciplinary proceedings, including monetary penalties and revocation or suspension of licenses or permits. The net effect of these reforms should be increased competition among brokers plus an acceleration in the licensing of customs brokers to operate as corporations.

Notes

1. Figures come from press releases of the Office of the U.S. Trade Representative. For background on the history and status of the U.S. steel industry, see U.S. House of Representatives, Committee on Ways and Means, *Problems of the U.S. Steel Industry.* 98th Congress, 2nd Session, Serial 98–93 (1984), and William T. Hogan, S.J., *Steel in the United States: Restructuring to Compete* (Lexington, Mass.: Lexington Books, 1984).

2. *Problems of the U.S. Steel Industry, op. cit.*, p. 108.

3. *Ibid.*, p. 162.

4. See U.S. International Trade Commission, *Carbon and Certain Alloy Steel Products*, Vol. 1. USITC Publication 1553 (July 1984), p. 3.

5. See chapter 6.

6. Figures of the Bureau of Labor Statistics, cited in *The Washington Post*, October 27, 1985.

7. The CRS study is cited in *Inside U.S. Trade*, November 1, 1985.

8. See "Non-Producers Ship Steel to U.S." in *The Washington Post*, November 12, 1985.

8
Conclusions and Developments since 1984

T he Trade and Tariff Act of 1984 is neither the first nor the last word in U.S. trade policy. Because it is primarily composed of amendments to existing trade statutes, it is more properly seen as part of continuing process of revision than as an autonomous legislative event. The preceding six chapters have discussed how several of the TTA's provisions were implemented during the legislation's first year. The purpose of this final chapter is to tie the disparate trends together and to present a brief view of possible future developments.

Trade Policy at a Crossroads?

In his lengthy study of executive-legislative relations in trade policy, Robert Pastor discerned a recurring "cry and sigh" syndrome in the postwar American policy pattern.[1] The liberal trade community periodically lets out a mournful cry that the system is put in grave danger by a resurgence of protectionism, only to be followed by a sigh of relief when the danger passes. Pastor might add the enactment of the Trade and Tariff Act of 1984 to the list of protectionist scares that have erupted in Washington; while the act falls short of free trade purism, it does not stray too far afield from the mainstream of liberal trade policy.

The question arises, is the "cry and sigh" syndrome a permanent element in the trade policy environment? As of this writing, trade has reemerged as a leading political issue for 1986. The cries of protectionism are shrill once again, and it does not appear inevitable that the cry will again be followed by a sigh. It is always difficult to gauge accurately the ultimate historical significance of current events, but the second term of the Reagan administration appears to mark a critical juncture for U.S. trade policy.[2] Depending on the outcome of an increasingly heated domestic political debate, the United States could either encourage or reverse a decline in the global trading system. The key questions for the near future are:

> Will the executive branch maintain its dominance in setting and pursuing U.S. objectives, or will the Congress pose a renewed challenge to executive ascendancy?
>
> Will the trend toward bilateral relations begin to crowd out the principles of multilateralism and unconditional most-favored-nation treatment?
>
> Will the GATT regain its position at the center of the international trading system, or will disputes among its members render it an anachronistic institution?

Two extreme cases illustrate the possible range of future developments. At the liberal trader's optimistic extreme, the key issues facing the GATT system will be resolved through a reinvigoration of the liberal, multilateral trading order. The Congress will grant the executive branch the negotiating authority it needs to bargain with other countries over tariff and nontariff barriers, while U.S. trading partners in both the industrialized and the developing regions will agree to inaugurate a new round of multilateral trade negotiations in the GATT. At the other extreme, some fear that the world trading system could continue to slide into a pattern of discriminatory and protectionist policies. A national consensus on U.S. trade priorities would be blocked by intramural political warfare between the executive and legislative branches, with the conflict exacerbated by partisan, regional, and sectoral tensions. Without responsible leadership for the international trade system, a new trade war could erupt.

Which of these polar scenarios is closer to the truth for the latter half of the 1980s? The answer depends largely, though not exclusively, on the actions taken by the United States. The passage and implementation of the TTA provides the Reagan administration with necessary but insufficient authority to carry out its plans for an eighth round of GATT negotiations. The legislation explicitly approves the administration's negotiating objectives in the new issues, but does not offer complete authority to ratify any bargains it might make with other nations to achieve these goals. If the United States is to preside over the inauguration of a new round, it must not only win the approval of its trading partners, but it must also establish a domestic consensus for the initiative. The repoliticization of trade policy makes this a tricky proposition.

The Repoliticization of Trade Policy

The Progressive's goal of "taking politics out of the tariff" can never be fully achieved, but great strides have been made toward this ideal in the past half century. The first landmark in the establishment of a liberal trading order was the Reciprocal Trade Agreements Act of 1934, followed by the founding of the

GATT and the seven rounds of multilateral trade negotiations held under its auspices. Partisan and regional politics slowed the advance of liberal trade, but as long as the gains from trade were apparent, protectionism held less appeal. The perceived strategic importance of a liberal trading system contributed to the depoliticization of trade policy. When it was felt that liberal trade helped to maintain international stability and prosperity, that the United States held a special responsibility for providing leadership in the free world, and that the United States was economically unchallenged, the complaints of domestic industries were less salient.

The relative decline of U.S. economic and political leadership in the 1970s and 1980s was accompanied by a renewed domestic interest in trade as a political issue. As described in the introductory chapter of this book, the congressional minority opposed to liberal trade policies grew in size and influence during the early 1980s. Enactment of the TTA in October 1984 did not settle the trade policy problem for the rest of the decade. Far from expressing a consensus view among all parties on the future course of U.S. trade policy, the TTA countenanced several hastily drawn compromises that satisfied neither liberal traders nor their opponents.

Paradoxically, trade policy became a much more prominent political issue in the pre-election year of 1985 than it had been during the presidential campaign of 1984. The political jockeying between the two parties, combined with the desire of some congressional Republicans to distance themselves from an unpopular White House position, combined to make trade one of the expected front issues of the 1986 election.

The issue could die down on its own if the U.S. trade balance rights itself, but as of this writing there is little sign of real improvement. The 1985 merchandise trade deficit is expected to exceed the record 1984 figure of $123.3 billion, with projections reaching into the neighborhood of $150 billion. The trade debate is fueled by events as well as numbers, and high profile controversies kept the issue in the public spotlight during 1985. Japan announced in March that it would maintain the voluntary restraints it had imposed on automobile exports in 1981, but would raise the ceiling by 25 percent. The American political reaction to this announcement was surprisingly hostile. Subsequent efforts by Prime Minister Nakasone to reduce his country's trade surplus with the United States were sceptically received both at home and in Washington.

The Reagan administration's efforts to hold the line against protectionism tended to encourage renewed calls for restrictive action. The USITC reversed its earlier position against import relief for the domestic footwear industry in June 1985, but President Reagan announced in August that he would reject the commission's recommendation that shoe imports be restricted. Denouncing protectionism as "destructionism," the president declared instead that the United States should concentrate its energies on opening foreign markets to U.S. exports. He directed the U.S. Trade Representative to initiate proceedings under section 301 against trade barriers in Brazil, Japan, and South Korea, while giving Japan and the European Community three months to open their markets for U.S. leather products and canned fruit, respectively. The White House announcement was clearly intended to deflect criticism of his footwear decision, and to signal Congress and foreign governments that the executive branch was willing to use its full authority to fight foreign restrictions.

The continuing pressure for import restrictions threatened to wrest power from the executive branch. Some feared a return to congressional ascendancy in the issue, which raised the specter of the Smoot-Hawley Tariff of 1930 and the attendant rush by U.S. trading partners to close their own borders in retaliation. Several Democrats and Republicans appeared ready to enter a protectionist bidding war to win voter approval in 1986. In the first session of the 99th Congress (1985), more than 400 trade-related bills and resolutions were introduced, the great majority of which would restrict U.S. imports. The most drastic proposals centered on import surcharges and unilateral quotas on textiles and apparel, while the subjects of other bills ranged from a complete reorganization of the trade policy bureaucracy down to import relief for U.S. beekeepers.

The Reagan administration attempted to reestablish executive control by simultaneously toughening its trade posture and taking macroeconomic action. While the administration had earlier been ideologically opposed to interference with free market forces, Treasury Secretary James Baker announced on September 22, 1985 that the United States would work in concert with the other members of the Group of Five (Federal Republic of Germany, France, Great Britain, and Japan) to intervene in currency exchanges in order to drive down the overvalued dollar. This turnaround was complemented by a commitment from the other industrialized countries to stimulate demand in their own domestic economies, and a plan presented the next month to the International Monetary Fund for new lending to debtor nations in the third world. The day after Secretary Baker's announcement, the White House followed suit by issuing a new trade policy white paper. The white paper shared the same commitment to liberal trade principles that was expressed in its 1981 predecessor, but with a harder edge. The 1981 paper had optimistically emphasized the gains from free trade, the positive steps that the administration hoped to promote, and the economic prosperity it expected in the near future. The 1985 paper took a harsher tone regarding foreign barriers to U.S. trade, while indicating that the administration was ready to "play hardball" by making greater use of section 301 and proposing a special $300 million export financing program to counter the export subsidies used by some trading partners.

The combined actions may have improved President Reagan's chances of repeating his comparatively successful 1984 legislative performance, but as of this writing the outcome is uncertain. The only things that seems clear are that the 99th Congress is intent on passing new trade legislation, that amendments to the trade-remedy laws appear to be more popular than drastic proposals such as an import surcharge, and that the White House agenda may only be a starting point. The elements are present for a trade package that could be as, or more, varied than the TTA, but the final outcome is impossible to determine. In the pages to follow, we discuss some of the more notable issues on which the trade debate currently hinges.

Trade Policy Initiatives in the 99th Congress

The possible elements for a trade package in the 99th Congress may be described under the three general headings we have used throughout this book: authority to negotiate and retaliate, amendments to the trade-remedy laws, and measures relating to specific products. Each of these topical areas is described below.

Authority to Negotiate and Retaliate

New GATT Negotiations. The Reagan administration's principal trade policy goal is to inaugurate an eighth round of multilateral trade negotiations within the GATT. Many members of Congress continued to be sceptical over the proposal for a new round in 1985, viewing attempts to initiate negotiations as a meaningless exercise as long as U.S. goals are not more firmly established. The opposition to a new round rests to some degree on the fact that the executive branch exercises much greater control over the course of trade negotiations than does the Congress, and some legislators fear that granting negotiating authority to the president is tantamount to abdicating control in trade policy. If and when the Congress does grant explicit MTN authority to the executive branch, it seems likely that Congress will attach strict negotiating objectives to the authority. The administration may not even be willing to accept the authority if it is included as part of an omnibus trade package that is weighed down with protectionist provisions.

If the Congress does not provide the executive with multilateral authority in the form that the White House desires, the executive branch could still take the first steps towards a new trade round. The key legal problem is the authority to ratify the agreements reached in a round, not the express permission to begin discussions. It is conceivable that the administration would delay its request for ratification authority until the pressure for import restrictions has died down— but this could be a long time coming. The viability of this approach depends largely upon congressional forbearance, which may be a slim reed for the executive branch.

While the Congress appeared to welcome any new executive assertiveness in using section 301, and many members would gladly extend the scope of the law, some legislators were concerned that the administration's policy was only a short-term public relations ploy. They hoped to amend the statute in ways that were not supported by the White House. From the executive's perspective, the most disagreeable proposals were those that would limit the president's discretion by requiring retaliation under certain circumstances. Some initiatives would demand action under section 301 if a barrier identified in the *National Trade Estimate* report were not eliminated within a certain period, while others would call for mandatory retaliation if the USTR found that another country engages in industrial targeting practices, and the USITC determined that these practices caused or threatened material injury to U.S. industries. The most commonly supported proposals would transfer authority in sections 301 from the president to the U.S. Trade Representative, with the chief executive retaining the power to veto any actions by the USTR. This proposal is discussed shortly.

The Generalized System of Preferences. While the 1984 renewal of the GSP was intended to put this issue to rest for eight years, some of the legislation proposed to the 99th Congress would make additional changes in the program. The most drastic initiatives would graduate the leading beneficiary nations from the GSP, as had been attempted during the 98th Congress. If this were to transpire, then the GSP would lose all value as a negotiating tool with the newly industrialized countries that are graduated. Other ideas occasionally expressed on Capitol Hill would make continued GSP eligibility contingent upon the beneficiary country's entry into a new GATT round, agreements to limit textile and apparel exports to the United States, or various other conditions. Now that the GSP has been tarred with the brush of reciprocity, all types of new eligibility requirements may be stuck to it.

Import Surcharge Proposals. The extreme alternative to giving the executive branch complete discretion in its authority to negotiate with the threat of retaliation is to make retaliation automatic by statute. The most conspicuous proposals in the 99th Congress for automatic retaliation against foreign countries would impose hefty import surcharges on some or all U.S. trading partners. The Trade Act of 1974 provides the president with the discretionary power to impose a temporary surcharge of up to 15 percent on imports in order to overcome balance of payments shortfalls—as allowed under the GATT—but many of the legislative proposals introduced in the 99th Congress would give the president little or no flexibility in applying a surcharge. Depending on the proposal, the surcharge might be applied in a nondiscriminatory fashion (that is, to all U.S. trading partners) or to just those countries that meet certain criteria. In many bills, the criteria are obliquely but deliberately drawn in a manner that singles out Japan for retaliation.

The surcharge proposals carried a special appeal for legislators because they had the apparent advantage of simultaneously achieving political and economic objectives. First, the very threat of passing such legislation was intended to prod the executive branch and its foreign counterparts into taking decisive action to reverse the U.S. trade deficit. Second, the proposals seemed tailor-made for solving both the budget and trade deficits in one fell swoop. The initial economic appeal later subsided, however, when a series of technical reports by government and private economists showed that, in all probability, a surchage would cause more harm than good for the U.S. economy. Following the release of these studies, the surcharge advocates tended to play up their political arguments more than their economic appeals.

The first surcharge proposals of the 99th Congress were introduced at the suggestion of the Motorola Corporation shortly after the legislative session began in January 1985, but the most notable bill was not introduced until six months later. The Trade Emergency and Export Promotion Act (H.R. 3035/ S. 1449) was introduced by leading Democrats on Capitol Hill, and would employ a complicated calculus to determine which "excessive surplus nations" would be subject to a 25-percent import surcharge for up to five years. As drafted by its sponsors, the legislation would initially apply a surcharge to products from Brazil, Japan, South Korea, and Taiwan, unless they swiftly reduced their trade surpluses with the United States. The legislation would provide for a limited degree of executive flexibility, by allowing the president to exempt any country that did not engage in unfair trade practices. The sponsors included this provision to allow free-trading Hong Kong to escape any penalties for its surpluses.

An automatic import surcharge is a blunt instrument that severely limits the executive branch's ability to deal with foreign governments, and the Reagan administration opposed the Democratic surcharge in the strongest possible fashion. Ambassador Clayton Yeutter, the newly appointed U.S. Trade Representative, denounced the proposal as "the wrong medicine for the wrong disease," and predicted that the proposal (if passed) would lead to retaliation, decreasing export markets for U.S. producers, inflation for U.S. consumers and industrial importers, delays or defaults in foreign loan repayments, and economic and political instability abroad. He urged instead that the Congress work with the administration to reduce the fiscal deficit, while providing the executive branch with sufficient authority to negotiate new agreements with U.S. trading partners. By late 1985, the momentum for an import surcharge seemed to have subsided.

Amendments to the Trade-Remedy Laws

Many of the proposals to amend the trade-remedy laws that were defeated in 1984 resurfaced in 1985, together with some other initiatives that were not considered during the 98th Congress. The general thrust of most proposals would be to reduce the discretion available to the executive branch in the execution of these statutes. The amendments came in three basic types: reorganization of administrative authority, expansion of the scope of foreign practices that are subject to action under the statutes, and technical changes in the procedures and investigative methods provided by the laws.

The most drastic proposals would reduce or eliminate the president's discretion in sections 201 and 301, by requiring that action be taken in certain circumstances. Several bills would transfer the final decision-making authority now held by the president under sections 201, 301, 337 (unfair trade practices), and 406 (disruptive imports from communist countries) to the U.S. Trade Representative, together with administrative control over the GSP. The purpose here would be to reduce the influence of federal agencies that might oppose taking strong action against U.S. trading partners, and to depoliticize the international repercussions of presidential action under the statutes.

Some of the more significant trade remedy proposals entertained by the 99th Congress would expand the scope of antisubsidy and antidumping laws. A natural resources subsidization proposal would extend the definition of subsidies to cover finished goods that are made from natural resource inputs when the inputs are available at lower costs in the home market than they are in export markets. The proposal would have the effect of making goods that are produced with natural gas, petroleum, timber, and other resources subject to CVDs if it can be shown that the prices charged for the inputs in the home market are kept artificially low. The proposal would have a potentially severe impact on some industries in Canada, Mexico, Saudi Arabia, and other resource-rich nations. The Reagan administration argues that this proposal would contravene the established rule that government programs or subsidies that are generally available throughout the economy are not subject to countervailing action, and that it would be in clear violation of the GATT and the Subsidies Code.

A "diversionary dumping" provision would make a parallel revision in the antidumping statute, by directing the ITA to examine the prices of allegedly dumped inputs that are used to produce the finished goods imported into the United States. This proposal is very similar to the "downstream dumping" provision that was advanced during the 98th Congress. It would define an end product to have been dumped if one of its principal components was sold to the producer at less than fair value. The Reagan administration argues that the proposal would unfairly burden producers of finished goods who have no control over the pricing practices of their suppliers and present tremendous practical difficulties to ITA investigators.

Several proposals have been advanced to make foreign industrial targeting practices explicitly subject to some or all of the trade-remedy statutes dealing with unfair imports, including section 301, the antidumping law, and antisubsidy legislation. Some bills would make industrial targeting an indicator of injury in USITC investigations under the escape clause.

Many of the technical amendments relating to the procedures and methods mapped out by the statutes would have a substantial impact on the operation of the trade-remedy laws. Among the proposals under consideration were amendments to eliminate preliminary determinations in certain AD and CVD investigations, reduce the causation standard in escape-clause cases from a "substantial cause" of serious injury to merely a "cause," providing "fast track" for perishable goods relief under the escape clause, giving the USTR the authority to extend provisional relief or retaliation under sections 201 and 301, allowing producers of components to have standing in trade-remedy cases involving finished goods, limiting the extension of the injury test in CVD cases involving countries that are not signatories to the GATT Subsidies Code, and making several adjustments in the definitional and procedural minutiae of the statutes.

Measures Relating to Specific Products

As a general rule, Capitol Hill has not enacted significant product-specific trade legislation since it passed the Smoot-Hawley Tariff Act of 1930. Following that final legislative revision of the tariff, virtually all congressional initiatives in trade policy have related to macro-policy issues rather than sectoral concerns. The few exceptions to this rule include very minor tariff revisions and reclassifications (such as those included in titles I and II of the TTA) and a handful of special laws such as the Steel Import Stabilization Act of 1984.

The 99th Congress saw a renewed interest in sectoral trade legislation. The single most important proposal was the Textile and Apparel Trade Enforcement Act (H.R. 1562/S. 680), which would establish tight restrictions on U.S. imports of textiles and apparel. The stated purpose of the sponsors was to enforce the provisions of the Multi Fiber Arrangement (MFA), under which textile-producing and -importing nations jointly agree to suspend the liberal trade priciples of the GATT in order to limit the growth of import penetration by developing countries in the markets of their industrialized competitors. The MFA is enforced through bilateral agreements and unilateral administrative actions.

Although the Reagan administration made great efforts during its first term to restrict imports of these products through strict enforcement of bilateral limits, the U.S. textile industry charged that skyrocketing imports were responsible for causing widespread layoffs and plant closings. The industry's allies in the Congress introduced legislation to roll back the level of permissible imports from major exporting countries to their 1981 levels, with minor growth rates allowed for the future. The effect of these rollbacks would be to reduce textile imports from most midlevel developing countries by about one-third. The legislation would exempt Canada and Europe from these draconian reductions, while providing marginally better growth levels for smaller suppliers.

The Reagan administration opposed the bill, stating instead that the United States should call for renewal of the MFA prior to its expiration in 1986. The administration was joined in its opposition by U.S. retail and import groups, as well as by many agricultural groups representing farmers who depend on open export markets. Opponents of the textile quota bill charged that the legislation would not enforce the MFA, but rather would repudiate U.S. obligations under the MFA and the bilateral agreements that had been negotiated under its auspices.

Together with the import surcharge legislation, the textile quota proposal became an instrument for exerting congressional pressure on the White House for a new hard-line trade policy. The proposal attracted a plurality of cosponsors in both houses, although in some instances the support was intended more to prod the president and please constituents than to promote unilateral restriction of the U.S. market. The legislation's sponsors hoped for a veto-proof margin of support, but were uncertain that the proposal would actually survive a show-down with the White House.

The Reagan administration was concerned not only by the textile legislation itself, but also by the potential for a snowball effect on Capitol Hill. The domestic footwear and copper industries succeeded in amending the textile bill with their own restrictive provisions. While these maneuvers made it even more likely that the bill would be vetoed by the president, they also won additional votes for the veto override. As expected, President Reagan vetoed this bill in December 1985, and it was not passed over the president's veto. By the end of the year, pressure for sectoral restrictions had given way to interest in the so-called "generic" proposals for amendments to the trade-remedy laws.

Conclusion

The ultimate significance of the Trade and Tariff Act of 1984 may be impossible to judge. Given the general continuity in U.S. trade law, policy, and practice, the contribution made by any single act of legislation cannot be easily isolated. The act certainly does not represent as fundamental a break from earlier patterns as did the Reciprocal Trade Agreements Act of 1934, nor is it as internally consistent as the Trade Act of 1974. Perhaps more than any other comprehensive trade act of the past half century, the TTA is the product of hastily drawn compromises and incomplete agendas. Those compromises are unlikely to endure for long.

Notes

1. Robert Pastor, *Congress and the Politics of U.S. Foreign Economic Policy 1929–1976* (Berkeley, California: University of California Press, 1980), especially chapter 6.

2. The hazards of writing history while it is still in the making can be illustrated by the case of E.E. Schattschneider, author of one of the great classics on the domestic politics of U.S. trade policy. Schattschneider's *Politics, Pressures and the Tariff* (New York: Prentice-Hall, 1935) described the political bargaining that led to the Smoot-Hawley Tariff of 1930 and the role of lobbies in the process. The book was published five years after the legislation was enacted and one year after it was amended by the historic Reciprocal Trade Agreements Act of 1934. Schattschneider misjudged the significance of the 1934 Act, and pessimistically concluded that U.S. trade policy would continue to be held hostage to protectionist special interests.

3. Office of the U.S. Trade Representative, "Administration Statement on International Trade Policy" (September 23, 1985), p. 9.

Index

Adjustment assistance (*see also* Escape clause), 101, 102, 105n.8
Afghanistan, 84
Agreement on Trade in Civil Aircraft, 151
Agricultural Adjustment Act of 1933, 17, 18
Agricultural trade (*see also* Common Agricultural Program; Wine), 8, 11, 14, 18, 20–21, 39, 46, 52, 54, 59, 63, 109, 118, 162
Agriculture, Department of, 17, 18, 98
Albania, 91n.34
American Association of Exporters and Importers, 19, 90n.18
American Federation of Labor–Congress of Industrial Organizations (AFL–CIO), 58, 78
Andean Group, 84
Antidumping Code, 7, 108
Antidumping duties (*see also* Steel; Trade-remedy laws), 19–20, 107–139, 143, 160–161; downstream or diversionary dumping, 110, 111, 138n.3, 160; persistent dumping, 20, 111, 119
Antigua, 77
Apparel. *See* Textiles and apparel
Argentina, 46, 91n.28
Association of South East Asian Nations (ASEAN), 15, 65, 84
Austria, 46
Automobiles (*see also* Japan), 2, 10, 31, 65, 155

Bahamas, 77
Bahrein, 87, 90n.26
Baker, James, 156
Baldrige, Malcolm, 110, 138n.5
Bangladesh, 80
Baucus, Max, 85
Belgium, 46
Bermuda, 87, 90n.26
Berne Convention, 34
Bethlehem Steel Corporation, 145
Bilateral negotiations (*see also* Generalized System of Preferences; Israel), 3, 5–6, 14–16, 28, 30, 31, 57–68, 127, 154
Brazil, 54, 72, 82–83, 90n.28, 110, 125–126, 137, 139n.17, 156, 159

Bread for the World, 88
Brock, William, 64, 72, 88, 110, 138n.5, 145
Brunei, 87, 90n.26
Bulgaria, 91n.34, 138n.4
Burke–Hartke legislation, 9

California, 59
Canada, 33, 110, 139n.17, 160, 161; free trade area with United States, 15, 36, 57, 65; trade disputes with the United States, 46, 51, 65, 120, 147, 150
Caribbean Basin Initiative, 11, 31, 58, 62–63, 67n.12, 77, 82, 88, 90n.26, 101, 151
Caribbean Community (CARICOM), 84
Carter, Jimmy, 46, 51, 102, 144
Chadha v. *Immigration and Naturalization Service* (*see also* Escape clause), 104
China (*see* People's Republic of China; Taiwan)
Common Agricultural Program, 20–21, 46
Communist countries (*see also* Export Administration Amendments Act of 1985; Section 406), 52, 67n.12, 138n.4; dumping cases and, 19, 110, 111, 138n.4; GSP and, 78, 83, 84, 91n.34
Compensation, 9, 14, 21, 39, 96, 98
Conditional most-favored-nation treatment. *See* Most-favored-nation
Congress: ratification of trade agreements, 3–4, 7, 9, 13, 22n.2, 59–60, 127; role in trade policy, 3–4, 9, 98, 104, 150, 154; 93rd Congress (1973–1974), 76; 97th Congress (1981–1982), 35, 38, 51; 98th Congress (1983–1984), 9, 12, 19, 20, 21, 22n.6, 34, 38, 51, 76–78, 103–104, 110–111, 118, 119–120, 127, 138n.4, 158, 159, 160; 99th Congress (1985–1986), 20, 128, 138n.3, 149, 150, 156–162
Congressional Research Service, 149
Consumers for World Trade, 19
Copper, 10, 21, 22, 85–86, 150, 162
Countervailing duties (*see also* Industrial targeting; Steel; Trade-remedy laws), 19–20, 41, 42, 107–139, 160–161; injury test, 16–17, 63, 109–110, 112, 161; natural resource subsidization, 19, 65, 110, 111,

137n.2, 160; upstream subsidization, 20, 111, 125–126, 128
Court of Appeals for the Federal Circuit, 115, 118, 135
Court of International Trade, 43, 111, 115, 116, 118–119, 124, 134–135, 136, 138n.4, 138n.6
Cuba, 91n.34
Customs Brokers Act of 1984, 151

Danforth, John C., 38, 40
Developing countries (*see also* Generalized System of Preferences), 7, 8, 20, 29, 31, 32, 43, 42, 109, 110, 127, 148, 156, 161
Dole, Robert, 38
Duties. *See* Tariffs.
Duty drawback, 134, 151

East Germany, 138n.4
Economic Policy Council, 98
Egypt, 57–58
El Salvador, 137n.1
Energy and Commerce Committee, 10, 34
Escape clause (*see also* Trade-remedy laws), 11, 16–17, 18, 22n.1, 41, 42, 95–106, 130, 160–161; amendments in 1984, 19, 103–104; cases, 46, 54, 85–86, 100, 102–104, 105n.4, 144–146, 155; compensation for invoking, 14, 96, 98–99
Ethiopia, 84
European Community (*see also* Common Agricultural Program), 39, 46, 54, 57, 58, 67n.12, 110, 118, 131, 139n.17, 143, 144, 146, 148, 156
Export Administration Amendments Act of 1985, 2, 138n.4

Federal Republic of Germany, 156
Finance Committee, 12, 15, 58, 60, 97, 105n.4
Footwear (*see also* Escape clause), 10, 21, 39, 54, 58, 71, 100, 103, 105n.4, 155, 162
Ford, Gerald R., 70, 71, 102
Foreign Assistance Act of 1961, 31
France, 36, 46, 50, 118, 156
Free trade areas. *See* Bilateral negotiations; Israel; Caribbean Basin Initiative
Friendship, Commerce and Navigation treaties, 5, 31, 37, 44, 58, 60, 64

General Accounting Office, 127, 139n.18
General Agreement on Tariffs and Trade (GATT; *see also* Multilateral trade negotiations), 6–9, 14, 15, 20, 27, 30, 70, 143, 154, 155, 158, 161; Article I, 37–38, 60, 70; Article VI, 108; Article XVI, 108; Article XIX, 95–96, 101–102; Article XXIII, 43; Article XXIV, 57, 59, 66n.1; codes, 7,

29, 43, 59; dispute-settlement procedures, 8, 11, 14, 43–45, 118; U.S. trade policy and, 8–11, 22n.3, 108–110, 111
Generalized System of Preferences (GSP), 1, 11, 12, 18, 22n.1, 57, 61, 69–91, 101, 160; competitive need limits, 72–73, 78, 82; graduation, 16, 69, 72–73, 74, 78, 158; new negotiability, 15–16, 28, 31, 35, 78–83, 158; rules of origin, 63, 75–76
Gibbons, Sam, 58, 67n.8
Guatemala, 46

Haiti, 77, 80
Hart, Gary, 145
Hawaii, 36
High technology, 11, 14, 27, 32–33, 151–152
Honduras, 77, 137n.1
Hong Kong, 72, 78, 80, 82, 90n.26, 91n.28, 110, 159
H.R. 3398, 12, 21
Hughes, Charles E., 5, 37
Hull, Cordell, 5
Hungary, 83

Import substitution, 32
Import surcharge, 158–159
Industrial targeting (*see also* Countervailing duties), 32, 33, 110, 126–128, 139nn.17–19, 158, 160
Injury test. *See* Antidumping duties, and countervailing duties)
Intellectual property rights (*see also* Section 337), 11, 14, 18, 27, 33–35, 52, 64, 77, 85
Internal Revenue Code, 51, 134
International Bank for Reconstruction and Development (World Bank), 6, 86
International Investment and Trade in Services Survey Act, 53
International Labor Organization, 85
International Monetary Fund, 6, 83, 156
International Trade Administration, 96, 98; role in AD and CVD cases, 16–20, 111–114, 120, 123–133, 135–137, 144, 147, 160
International Trade and Investment Act of 1984, 27, 40
International Trade Organization, 6, 9, 13, 30, 70
Investment, 11, 14, 27, 30–32, 38, 40, 48, 52, 77; performance requirements, 29, 31, 35, 49, 64, 86
Israel: Free trade area with the United States, 11–12, 15, 30, 35, 57–64, 101; GSP and, 57, 61, 72, 90n.26, 91n.28
Italy, 50, 118

Jackson–Vanik Amendment, 138n.4
Jamaica, 77

Japan, 32, 33, 38, 39, 110, 127, 139n.17, 156; automobile export restraints, 2, 11, 155; trade disputes with the United States, 51, 54, 124, 143, 144, 145, 149, 156, 158–159

Labor–Industry Coalition for International Trade (LICIT), 139n.17
Laos, 91n.33
Less developed countries. See developing countries
Liberia, 137n.1
Local-content rules. See Investment, performance requirements)
Lome agreements, 67n.12

Material injury. See Antidumping duties; Countervailing duties
Matsushita v. United States (see also Court of International Trade), 116–117, 136
Mexico, 15, 51, 72, 82, 91n.28, 109, 126, 137, 139n.17, 160
Mondale, Walter, 145, 146
Most-favored-nation (MFN; see also General Agreement on Tariffs and Trade; Jackson–Vanik Amendment): conditional MFN, 3–4, 36–37, 60, 64; exceptions to, 8, 38, 57, 58, 66, 67n.12, 70, 110, 138n.4; unconditional MFN, 5, 6, 10, 29, 33, 36–38, 47, 110, 154
Motorola Corporation, 159
Multi Fiber Arrangement. See Textiles and apparel
Multilateral trade negotiations: 7, 21, 53, 54, 155; authority and ratification, 5–6, 13–14, 58; Kennedy Round, 7, 108; new round, 11–15, 29, 35, 58, 154, 157–158; Tokyo Round, 7, 13, 14, 39, 43, 44, 59, 70, 81, 108; U.S. objectives in, 11, 12–16, 30, 32, 33, 35

Nakasone, Yasuhiro, 155
National Trade Estimate. See Section 301
National treatment, 29, 31, 32, 47, 49, 64
Natural resource subsidization. See Countervailing duties
Nauru, 87, 90n.26
Nepal, 137n.1
New issues. See High technology; Intellectual property rights; Investment; Services
Newly industrialized countries, 14, 16, 72, 158
Nonmarket economies. See Communist countries
Nontariff barriers, 7, 14, 29, 31, 32, 46, 59
North Korea, 91n.33
North Yemen, 137n.1

Office of the U.S. Trade Representative (USTR), 61, 96, 98, 105n.4, 120, 127, 139n.19; role in Section 301, 41–46,

155–156, 158, 161; GSP and, 71, 73, 160; Trade Policy Committee, 52, 98
Orderly marketing agreements, 7, 98, 101, 144
Organization for Economic Cooperation and Development, 29, 30, 109
Organization of Petroleum Exporting Countries, 83, 84

Panama, 77
Paris Convention for the Protection of Industrial Property, 34
Pastor, Robert, 153
Patent Cooperation Treaty, 34
Pease, Donald J., 81
People's Republic of China, 91n.34
Performance requirements. See Investment
Presidential authority in trade policy (see also Section 301), 16, 43, 48, 71, 79, 87, 96–99, 100, 101, 102–103, 104, 133, 147, 158, 160
Puerto Rico, 151

Quotas, 17, 35, 40, 101, 102

Reagan, Ronald W., 46, 58, 85, 102, 162
Reagan administration trade policy, 11–12, 14, 15, 19, 21, 29, 40–41, 52, 54, 76, 110–111, 118, 132, 133, 144–146, 147, 153–154, 156–157, 159, 160, 161
Reciprocal Trade Agreements Act of 1934, 5–6, 9, 13, 37, 154, 162, 163n.2
Reciprocity (see also Generalized System of Preferences; Retaliation; Section 301): code reciprocity, 7, 38, 109–110, 158; history of, 35–38; "new" reciprocity, 38–41; sectoral reciprocity, 39, 40, 50–51
Retaliation (see also Section 301), 9, 32, 39, 45–46, 48, 49–50, 53, 96, 101, 110, 127, 158, 159
Rostenkowski, Dan, 138n.5, 146
Rules of origin. See Generalized System of Preferences; Israel

Saudi Arabia, 160
Schattschneider, E.E., 163n.2
Section 22. See Agricultural Adjustment Act of 1933
Section 201. See Escape clause
Section 301, 14–15, 19, 22n.1, 27, 30, 35, 40, 41–55, 127, 130, 144, 149, 156, 160–161; National Trade Estimate, 51–53, 86, 158; proposals in the 99th Congress, 127–128, 157–158; self-initiation of cases, 49, 54–55, 155–156
Section 337 (see also Intellectual property rights), 17–18, 34, 160
Section 406 (see also Communist countries), 17–18, 138n.4, 160
Semiconductor Chip Protection Act of 1984, 34

Services, 11, 14, 27, 28–30, 38, 40, 48, 52, 53, 63–64, 86
Shamir, Yitzhak, 58
Sharon, Ariel, 64
Singapore, 72, 80, 82, 87, 90n.26
Smoot–Hawley Tariff Act of 1930, 151; as tariff protection, 5, 6, 138n.4, 156, 161, 163n.3; trade-remedy sections, 17, 22n.1, 34, 107, 108, 116, 124–125, 134
South Korea, 46, 51, 54, 72, 78, 80, 82, 90n.26, 91n.28, 110, 139n.17, 145, 149, 156, 159
Spain, 137
Steel, 10, 39, 65, 71, 78; AD and CVD cases, 19, 46, 115, 122, 125, 131, 137, 143; escape clause cases, 11, 102, 105n.4; Fair Trade in Steel Act of 1984, 144–145; Steel Import Stabilization Act of 1984, 2, 12, 21, 143–150, 161
Subsidies. *See* Countervailing duties
Subsidies Code (*see also* countervailing duties), 38, 44, 64, 108–110, 125, 126, 129, 160, 161
Surcharge. *See* Import surcharge
Sweden, 46

Taiwan, 51, 72, 78, 80, 82, 90n.26, 91n.28, 109, 139n.17, 159
Targeting. *See* Industrial targeting
Tariff Act of 1890, 36
Tariff Act of 1897, 36–37
Tariff Act of 1930. *See* Smoot–Hawley Tariff
Tariff Schedules of the United States (TSUS), 21, 150–151
Tariffs (*see also* Multilateral trade negotiations; Smoot–Hawley Tariff), 3–8, 13, 29, 32, 52, 101, 102; effect of low rates on GSP, 16, 70, 71
Textile and Apparel Trade Enforcement Act of 1985, 161–162
Textiles and apparel, 3, 8, 9, 156; GSP and, 71, 158; Israeli free trade area and, 58, 62; Multi Fiber Arrangement, 2, 10, 20, 62, 161; Reagan administration policy, 11, 161–162
Tokyo Round. *See* Multilateral trade negotiations
Trade Act of 1974, 9, 13, 14, 18, 22n.1, 41, 42, 44, 47, 59–60, 67, 69, 70, 71, 77, 79, 83, 95, 96, 98, 102, 104, 108, 138n.4, 158, 162
Trade Agreements Act of 1979, 48, 108, 121, 130
Trade Emergency and Export Promotion Act, 159
Trade Policy Committee. *See* Office of the U.S. Trade Representative

Trade Reform Action Coalition, 19
Trade Remedy Assistance Center, 119–120
Trademark Counterfeiting Act of 1984, 34
Trademarks. *See* Intellectual property
Trade-remedy laws (*see also* Antidumping duties; Countervailing duties; Escape clause; Industrial targeting; Section 301; Section 337), 1, 7, 9, 16–20, 74, 159–161; GATT and, 8–9, 108–111, 125, 160; politics of, 9–12, 110–111, 154–156, 159–161
Trading with the Enemy Act of 1917, 2
Trautlein, Donald, 145
Treasury (*see also* James Baker), 98
Trinidad and Tobago, 51, 90n.26

Union of Soviet Socialist Republics (*see also* Communist countries), 46, 138n.4
Unions. *See* American Federation of Labor–Congress of Industrial Organizations
United Kingdom, 3, 46, 156
United Nations Conference on Trade and Development (UNCTAD), 69, 70
Upstream subsidization. *See* Countervailing duties
U.S. Chamber of Commerce, 19, 76, 90n.18
U.S. Customs Service, 2, 22, 88, 114, 129, 133, 134, 146, 149, 151
U.S. International Trade Commission, 22n.1, 34, 42, 61, 63, 86, 103–104, 105n.1, 128, 158; AD and CVD cases, 16–17, 112–115, 120–123, 135; escape clause and, 96–97, 99–101, 144, 155; GSP and, 70, 72, 74, 79, 80; U.S. Tariff Commission, 5, 37
USTR. *See* Office of the U.S. Trade Representative

Venezuela, 91n.33, 137n.1
Vietnam, 91n.34
Voluntary restraint agreement. *See* Escape clause; Steel

Ways and Means Committee, 10, 15, 21, 58, 60, 76, 97, 105n.4, 138n.5, 146
Weintraub, Sidney, 66, 67n.12
White papers on trade policy: 1981 paper, 11, 27, 31, 66, 156; 1985 paper, 66, 156
Wine: AD and CVD cases, 117–119; Wine Equity and Export Expansion Act of 1984, 50–51
World Bank. *See* International Bank for Reconstruction and Development
World Intellectual Property Organization, 34
World War II, 6

Yeutter, Clayton, 53, 76, 159

About the Authors

Stephen L. Lande is an international trade expert and a professional negotiator. As vice-president of Manchester Associates, Ltd., an international business consulting firm, Mr. Lande has been an advisor to several U.S. and foreign corporations, governments, and international organizations. Before assuming his present position, he served as assistant United States Trade Representative, where he was responsible for bilateral relations with developing countries and Japan, implementation of the GSP, and the development of the Caribbean Basin Initiative. Prior to joining USTR, Mr. Lande served as a Foreign Service Officer in the State Department. He received a B.A. degree in economics from Colgate University and an M.A. degree in international economics from the Johns Hopkins School of Advanced International Studies. Mr. Lande currently is an adjunct professor for international trade in the Landegger Program in International Business Diplomacy of Georgetown University.

Craig VanGrasstek is president of VanGrasstek Communications, a Washington-based consulting firm specializing in U.S. trade policy. He has been a consultant to the Agency for International Development, the Bureau of Intelligence and Research of the State Department, the General Secretariat of the Organization of American States, the Korean Traders Association, the Latin American Economic System, the United Nations Conference on Trade and Development, and the governments of Costa Rica, Haiti, Honduras, Mexico, Quebec, and Singapore. Mr. VanGrasstek is also a freelance journalist whose articles have appeared in *International Management*, the *Journal of Commerce*, *Time Magazine*, and the *Washington Post*. His recent publications include a chapter in *Central America and the Western Alliance* (Washington, D.C.: Carnegie Endowment for International Peace, 1985) and a chapter written with Stephen Lande in *U.S. Foreign Policy and the Third World: Agenda 1985–86* (Washington, D.C.: Overseas Development Council, 1985). He holds a master's degree from Georgetown University's School of Foreign Service, and was a Fulbright Scholar at the University of the Andes in Bogotá, Colombia.

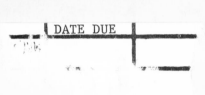